VICTORIANA

By the same author:

DOLLS' HOUSES: A PERSONAL CHOICE

Papier-mâché inkstand and blotter; *surround, from top left,* head inkwell; pounce pot; Staffordshire quill holder; French paperweight *c.* 1840; bellows pencil; pipe inkwell and pen; hand paperclip; cat penwiper; hand weight; wheel of seals; pipe propelling pencil; French paperweight *c.* 1840

Jean Latham

VICTORIANA

STEIN & DAY/*Publishers*/New York

First published in the United States of America by
Stein and Day/Publishers 1971
Copyright © 1971 Jean Latham
Library of Congress Catalog Card No. 76-148833

Printed in Great Britain
Stein and Day/Publishers7/ East 48 Street, New York, N.Y. 10017
SBN: 8128-1372-3/

CONTENTS

CONTENTS

ILLUSTRATIONS

ACKNOWLEDGEMENTS

My thanks to the Director of *Collectors' Guide* for allowing me to use some photographs from articles I wrote for them and also for permission to quote certain passages from them where relevant. Thanks also to the following museums for letting me illustrate sections from their collections:

The Victoria and Albert Museum; Peterborough Museum; Harris Museum and Art Gallery, Preston; Fitzwilliam Museum, Cambridge; Science Museum, S.W.7; Musée d'Histoire de l'Education; Tunbridge Wells Museum; Museum of Childhood, Edinburgh.

Also thanks to Miss Fanny Foster for her great grandmother's picture and to Mr Anthony Oliver for permission to quote from his illuminating articles in *Collectors' Guide*, August, September and October 1969 issues; to my photographer Mr Llewellyn Robins, of Studio Wreford, Marlborough, who photographed items from my collection and gratitude and thanks to Miss Grace Cansdale for once more tackling the typing of my difficult manuscript.

INTRODUCTION

The Victorians had an insatiable hunger for living, and that meant that they laughed loudly and cried immoderately and were certainly not afraid of their emotions. Such novelists of the period as Dickens and Thackeray bear witness to this. The home in all its stability was extremely important, and the Family Man symbolized the prosperity and security of the rising, prosperous middle-class. The Industrial Revolution at first led to poverty and unemployment, but by the 1830s it began to bring in such dividends as the railway system, increased travel and better roads. By 1840 hanging was a penalty imposed only for murder, and although the sufferings of the poor continued, there were reformers, among them the Prince Consort himself, who interested themselves in the improvement of living and working conditions, as well as in education and hospitals.

Against this background the importance of family life meant larger homes, more and more servants for the well-to-do and an increasing interest in acquiring possessions. The Victorians were great collectors of *bric-à-brac*, what with the scrap screens, the vases of pampas-grass, the innumerable daguerrotypes of all the members of their huge families, jostling for place with flowers made of wax or muslin, shells and wool enshrined beneath dust-proof glass shades. There were also the face-screens, the blotters, the boxes of all kinds and the lovely gay-coloured glass vases, striped, spangled, iridescent and opaline.

Perhaps not a bad way to start searching for Victoriana is to see the humour, not always intentional, in some of the strange but often

11

endearing assortment of things to be seen in every antique shop in our country nowadays, except of course the splendid ones aiming at the rich connoisseurs, which do not concern us here.

When we collect, what we are really doing is to acquire small pieces of history, which is why no serious collector can ignore the history of his chosen period. A study of the times when the objects for which we are searching were made is absolutely essential for a full appreciation of them, and in the case of Victoriana the period covers three-quarters of a century.

During the reign of Victoria the population of England and Wales doubled. The result was that the working-classes had a very thin time of it, children of ten being sent out to work because pay was so inadequate, and even up until 1900 a large part of our nation was still living at subsistence level. These unpalatable facts we tend to ignore, as of course the middle and upper classes were doing very nicely, thank you. The average father of the family dominated the gentle, submissive wife, who expected to be guided through all the storms of life by her well-to-do-husband, and in return she provided him with an enormous quiverful of children. Needlework, embroidery, social visits and very little housework was the lot of the richer Victorian wife, and it was not until the beginning of the twentieth century that women began seriously to rebel against this cramped, unintelligent life.

The objects we collect today under the portmanteau word Victoriana were the things that decorated the homes of these middle-class families. Much of it was made by the mother and her daughters, the maiden aunts and the helpful governess. They became extremely adept at the various crafts and the results are often delightful, decorative and beautifully made. The beadwork, the needlework pictures and needle-work chaircovers, the embroidered cushions, bell-pulls and mats; the shellwork boxes, pictures, hand-mirror frames, dolls dressed in shells; the hand-worked flounces, valences, antimacassars and, of course, the exquisitely stitched handkerchiefs and underclothes. All these were home-made.

In 1886 a significant event occurred. The Shop Hours Act made it illegal for children under the age of eighteen to do more than seventy-four hours work a week. They need only work thirteen-and-a-half hours a day and on Saturdays six-and-a-half. What leisure and freedom this meant is hard for us, with our forty-hour week, to contemplate.

A Victorian surgeon wrote in his journal in 1842 about Sunday in Battersea Fields, with the thousands of working-class families strolling about and drinking at the beer-shops. No music was allowed then on a Sunday so drinking and smoking was all they could enjoy. But, of course, there were the sands and beaches for days out and holidays. The Victorians adored paddling. This suggests another line of Victoriana in picture postcards, today much in demand, and the fairings sold to the trippers, which were made in great quantities on the Continent and shipped over to England. The go-to-bed groups, the pin-boxes and match strikers are examples of this sort of quarry for the collector, not to mention the toys for a penny or two in the many bazaars and those also being sold in the itinerant pedlars' trays.

Collectors of Victoriana find that one thing leads to another. A tropical sea shell carved with a cameo brings an interest in associated seaside attractions such as the Alum Bay coloured sands in bells or birds or lighthouses. This leads to sand pictures, copying a Japanese invention, or to shell pictures, especially those made by Jane Parminter, and wool pictures of ships, paperweights with seaside views, etchings or water-colours of the sea. John Leech sketched a charming scene of huts and bathing girls at Sandbath. Staffordshire pottery figures can be included, like the Scottish herring lassie. A lithographed songsheet of shells and seaweed is called "Sea Shells Polka", and seaweed pictures were another popular craft of Victorian times. These are the small change of Victoriana, the real *bric-à-brac*.

As you can see the scope is enormous, so in the following pages we will look further and in greater detail at a selection of the many different collectors' items now classified as Victoriana. But it should be borne in mind that this is not a standard work, merely an appetizer to suggest a few of the collectable things to be found under the umbrella-term of Victoriana, which, after all, covers three-quarters of a century.

J.L.

POTTERY

1

Castles and Cottages

Few other antiques have quite the same power to evoke the age in which they were made as the charming little pastille burners, overgrown with outsize flowers, and representing dreamlike cottages, toll houses, arbours for lovers and dovecotes, not to mention churches and turreted castles. The most prized of them were made in delicate porcelain by Coalport, Rockingham and Derby, Spode, Worcester and other factories. They reflect the romantic "age of the grotto" when Georgian ladies and gentlemen built themselves Gothic cottages or "aweful" ruins in their parks. These fanciful cottages *ornées* and the castles with their toy turrets and pinnacles were meant for the sophisticated homes. Architects of the time were building extraordinary fancies like Beckford's nightmare Abbey of Fonthill, or Walpole's Strawberry Hill. Horace Walpole, who died as late as 1814, used to warn his friends that his "Gothick" mansion was so small that he could "wrap it up and enclose it in the letter he was writing". It sounds remarkably like its counterpart in porcelain.

The cottage pastille burners, made in both pottery and porcelain, were produced in the eighteenth century to a lesser extent than in the nineteenth. They are said to have originated in the Netherlands at the end of the seventeenth century. Dutch William and Mary II were much in favour of blue and white wares, it seems, and there is a blue and white pastille burner marked 1691. English slipware examples were being made early in the eighteenth century and their ancestors, the open vessels called essence pots or casolettes, were used as far back as the Renaissance. After 1820 and until the middle of Victoria's reign the pastille burners were being made in their hundreds in porcelain and in pottery, so that they ornamented the homes of rich and poor alike.

In the badly ventilated rooms of Regency days, with their low standards of cleanliness, the little cones, made out of powdered charcoal and gum arabic mixed with various delicious perfume oils, were invaluable. The cones were lit inside the china cottages and a spiral of sweet-smelling smoke helped to mask the less acceptable odours of the stuffy rooms.

The earlier little cottage windows looked out on to a world of gentlemen with wigs or powdered hair—Lord Bathurst did not cut off his pigtail until 1828—a world so melodramatic at the beginning of the nineteenth century that in Kensington a bell used to be rung on Sunday evening to assemble the revellers from London so that they might walk home together in safety lest robbers or highwaymen attack them.

About 1840 a non-guttering candle was invented and the cottages gradually changed function to become nightlight holders. Roofs and walls could be lifted off in one piece, though sometimes only the roof comes off. Money-boxes vary from the early blue and white ones, made in Staffordshire, to the shiny, treacly ones often attributed to Rockingham. Few of all these little extravagances are marked, though many fakes have impressive gold anchors to trap the unwary into thinking they are Chelsea. Sometimes they have the Leeds mark or the crown of Derby.

Attributions are not easy, but a few tips may help. Recent research suggests that a good deal of what has passed for Rockingham may not be so. Rockingham potters, however, are thought to have used the pink convolvulus on their roofs a good deal; they were also fond of a soft mauve, though this was copied in Staffordshire. If a mark is found on a Rockingham piece it will be that of Brameld; a red griffin

Castles and Cottages: a mansion, cottage and chalet attributed to Rockingham, mid-nineteenth century; *bottom left*, a castle, possibly intended as a candle-holder, Staffordshire

Left, ravens in the belfry, a rare piece
of Staffordshire china; *below*, early
nineteenth-century cottage with slot
behind chimneys for pennies

indicates the period 1826–30, one in puce 1830–42. If you find an impressed X, that also is probably Rockingham.

Large sweet peas, carnations and ranunculus are said to come from Coalport; violets and primroses, exquisitely painted and picked out in gold lines, are likely to indicate Worcester, some of whose houses stand on little feet. Derby and Wedgwood both made a very similar biscuit porcelain; do look out for enchanting, small, misty-blue cottages encrusted with white flowers which come from Wedgwood.

Large heavy cottages meant for decorating mantelpieces had a great vogue from 1825 until about 1850. Some are 10 inches high and the churches can be as much as 14 inches tall. Night light cottages were big, too, sometimes. About 1830 Grainger Lee and Co. produced some 8 inches high and Minton made large ones with a delightful bird perched on the roof.

Besides all these little miniature properties with specific functions like money-boxes, pastille-burners, or even doorstops and tobacco jars, tea-caddies and teapots, many cottages were made simply for ornaments. These were mostly chimney-ornaments and are particularly associated with the reign of Queen Victoria, moreover they were usually pottery and these, from Sussex and Staffordshire and the Northern counties, make a delightful collection in themselves. A charming ruined castle, found recently, has been built on a bridge encrusted with flowers and two swans float on the river beneath it. The ruins are occupied by a family of ravens, or are they rooks peeping out of the windows? Collectors could limit themselves to a subject; castles, for instance, or what about collecting crime pieces?

The sinister red of the barn at Polestead, in Essex, where the villainous William Corder murdered Maria Marten, the daughter of a Suffolk mole catcher in 1828, chills the spine even now. Stanfield Hall is a stately moat-surrounded mansion where James Rush, a regular bull of a man to judge by his pottery image, came from his neighbouring flower-bedecked home, Potash Farm, to polish off the ill-fated Isaac Jermy and his son. These houses, together with a rare piece representing Norwich Castle, where Rush paid the penalty of his crimes in 1849, could start a handsome collection; not forgetting Palmer's House, *circa* 1856, the home of the poisoner and one-time house surgeon at Bart's.

There are also figures of the various actors in these dramatic scenes for your gallery of rogues. Whieldon's plaque is probably the earliest, inspired by Hogarth's engraving of Sarah Malcolm, who was executed in 1733 for three murders. There is a splendid Charlotte Corday assassinating Marat in 1793, on a rectangular simulated-marble plinth, which is in the Fitzwilliam Museum, Cambridge.

Cream or white porcelain cottages are another suggestion. Minton made some large ones very well modelled too, and they have one touch of colour in a goldfinch perched charmingly on the roof. There is also a series of cottages with an opening to hold a watch.

Needless to warn the wary collector that copies of both porcelain and pottery cottages abound, but it seems as though they lack some indefinable delicacy of touch and the distinction of the early work. Compare a known reproduction with a genuine old one and you will see at once the difference.

The range is enormous and the prices are equally varied. The Red Barn fetched over £100 in London a few years ago; yet I found a tiny, shrimp-coloured, ruined castle pastille burner only a few months ago for fifteen shillings. So bargains are still available.

2

Children's Gift Plates

A collection of these delightful gifts for good boys and girls, some of which have "Present for a good girl" inscribed on them, are colourful and gay enough to hang on the walls, to display on the kitchen dresser or mantelpiece, or even in the living-room.

Nineteenth-century children were lucky to have these enchanting plates made specially for them in great variety. Some are only in monochrome of green, blue, black or sepia but many were decorated with rhymes and pictures, which help us to date their first appearance. Of course the plates might have been re-issued by the factories of their origin for years, so as they were practically never marked we can only date them approximately, though many signs can help identification as to which factory made them. It is surprising that so many have survived the rough and tumble of nursery life.

Tommy Thumb's Pretty Song-book, dated 1744, is believed to be the earliest book of collected nursery rhymes, but the earliest child's plate I have come across is at least twenty years later. We must not confuse these gift plates with the traveller's samples, the dolls' services or the dolls' house sets. These children's plates were designed to "elevate, amuse or interest" the young, and they were generally made of earthenware and not, as might have been expected, of the much stronger stoneware which is very hard and non-porous. Earthenware is much cheaper to produce and has been called "the poor man's porcelain".

Years ago the country potter was a feature of village life and the craft passed from father to son, the wares being taken to market perhaps on a pack-horse or bumped along the rough roads in a cart. No doubt the plates met with very rough treatment even before they reached their first buyer, who might be the "image-seller" or some other itinerant shopkeeper, who hawked his stock from one village to another. The plates were made chiefly in the potteries of Tyneside, Staffordshire and Sunderland as well as in Scotland, and also in Swansea. They vary in size from about 4½ inches in diameter to as much as 9 inches.

Anyone who has access to a helpful public library should ask to look at the monumental and fully illustrated standard work by Morton Nance called *Pottery and Porcelain of Swansea and Nantgarw*. Detailed pictures and descriptions of many of these "gift plates for children with embossed bird and flower borders" help the collector to identify his finds.[1]

The embossed borders were very popular at Swansea and appear on many dinner services. Look out for embossed alphabets, daisies and bright-coloured roses and tulips in purply-blues, chrome pink and dark green, with black or sepia transfer pictures in the centre of the plate. Some early plates come in delightful Pratt colourings of the distinctive orange-yellow, Indian red and apple-green. I have a plate of this type impressed Dixon-Austin, which dates it between 1810 and 1820. It comes from the Sunderland pottery. This is, of course, a little early for Victoriana, but in a collection it is often interesting to include the early forerunners of your subject, though the *early* children's plates are neither cheap nor easy to find, being so very "collectable".

The variety, however, is wide enough for most of us to find interesting additions to our collection. A transfer-printed series of the Ages of Man, a zoological series and another of birds encircled by brightly coloured flowers, all come from Swansea, while a geographical series with views of Canada and America are dated 1850. There is an amusing series of children's games, and one shows an

[1]The Glamorgan Pottery, Swansea, produced some particularly fine, richly coloured early examples.

attractive little girl "Jumping the Rope". Quite a number of these gift plates have alphabets moulded in the rim or painted in the centre of the plate, and many are either instructive or moral in their inscriptions.

The simplest of these plates are the rather thick pottery examples, decorated with embossed daisies, a characteristic border of Swansea and also the Don Pottery in Yorkshire which uses daisies in several rows, as well as the Bramelds of Rockingham, who designed both a green glaze jug, for example, and a caneware jug covered with these flowers. These plates have alphabets or formal patterns round the rims as well as the daisies, and the transfer pictures are simply in black, blue, green or sepia. Many of them come from Tyneside and date mostly from about 1831 to 1850. The octagonal plates, some with a line of lustre round their edges and colour roughly painted on the transfers, make a pleasant contrast to the round ones.

Collectors anxious to confine themselves only to marked examples of these pretty plates can sometimes find the marks of William Smith & Co., a firm in Stockton-on-Tees. "W. S. & Co." appears printed or impressed and sometimes the full name can be found. Geoffrey A. Godden notes that German inscriptions appear on some of this firm's children's plates, and he points out that this shows the firm exported these plates; I have found French examples as well. Mr. Godden adds that the words "Wedgwood" (or "Wedgewood") or "Queens Ware" occur frequently on these Stockton examples.[1] Bailey and Ball of Longton is another firm making children's plates; the octagonal shape with its moulded border design is theirs, Mr. Godden tells us. The design was registered in March 1847, as were many designs both for the printed pattern and for moulded edges to the plates and dishes. Registered designs, marked with the diamond sign which exactly dates the article, are found on many pieces of Victorian ceramics and some collectors specialize in these alone. Another interesting fact is that the British Registration mark was also used by foreign firms and the agents for the sale of certain designs in England.

[1] *Antique China and Glass under £5*, by Geoffrey A. Godden. (Arthur Barker Ltd.)

Children's mugs belong to the same category of country-fair items made at small potteries, and these can be added to the gift plates most advantageously.

Queen Victoria and her husband and children figure on both mugs and gift plates. These are often very decorative and sometimes of superior potting in china. The mugs were often inscribed with children's names or initials, which may point to their having been "bespoke" gifts.

3

Collectable Lions

The collector of lions has an enormous choice from all sorts of materials including glass, porcelain, pottery and wood, metals and stone, not to mention all those that figure in paintings, drawings, tapestries and textiles. Naturally there are a considerable number of lions which are decidedly non-collectable, but we need not exert ourselves to make an inventory of those.

Besides being our national beast, the lion seems to have fired the imagination of mankind throughout history, and we have hunted him, befriended him, tamed him and even harnessed him. In heraldry he is the symbol of power and sovereignty. The personal quarterly coat of arms of the Queen as sovereign shows six lions walking, or passant, and one Scottish lion rampant.

A magnificent pair of faience lions from the factory at Lunéville in Lorraine fetched 750 guineas at Christie's a few years ago. These were a very unusual type, with black faces, blue eyes and open red mouths. Decorative they certainly were, though their demoniac expressions might well alarm the timorous. There are also lions from Lunéville with a rather more friendly aspect which are bright blue all over with red mouths. A pair of terracotta lions, made by the eighteenth-century sculptor Canova about 1790, was sold recently for £620. Probably models for those watching over Clement XIII's tomb, they were a little under 6 inches long. It is not size that counts in the world of collecting, of course, but lions certainly show an enormous range, from these little terracotta beasts to the huge stone animal from Waterloo station which now graces Westminster Bridge.

Pottery and porcelain lions are among the most popular, and they are very often in pairs. We can look for the homely brown Staffordshire lion, a mere chimney ornament, for instance, who stands beside a tree-stump spill-holder. This friendly creature has that comical, round-eyed human face we associate with Staffordshire lions of all kinds. Not only is it much cosier to look at than the splendid Lunéville pair, but it is also unlikely to strain our resources so much. The Staffordshire potters also produced a pair of lions holding down the recumbent figure of Napoleon III in an ignominious position. This was made during the scare in 1860 of war between ourselves and the French. Another historical figure worth looking out for is the Death of the Lion Queen. Poor Ellen Bright, mauled by a tiger in her uncle George Wombwell's menagerie in 1850, is immortalized in a Staffordshire group representing the lady with a lion on one side and the rogue tiger on the other. Incidentally, a sleeping lion lies on uncle George Wombwell's tomb in Highgate cemetery, London.

The lion modelled in various materials with one paw on a globe was inspired by a Florentine lion and was very popular in Regency days. There is one of pinkish-brown pottery in the Victoria and Albert Museum, probably made at Burslem about 1800. It is standing on a simulated marble plinth decorated with leaves of turquoise blue. This animal has an attribution saying "after the bronze lion in the Loggia dei Lanzi in Florence". The Leeds factory made this model in several sizes, the largest being 12 inches long, and Bow produced one in porcelain as early as the 1750s. The Scottish Portobello factory acquired by Thomas Rathbone at the beginning of the nineteenth century is especially associated with its handsome lions, copied from the Florentine originals.

Considering the lion's position as our national beast, it is not very surprising he should feature so much in our art. They appear as knobs on teapots, tobacco jars and other boxes and are used decoratively on furniture. Brass lion's-head handles, for instance, with a ring in the mouth, were popular in many periods. Some eighteenth-century furniture shows a leg with the lion's head at the knee and a ball-and-claw foot. Boulle used lion mask handles during the reign of Louis XIV and lions are also used on François I furniture. Leonine doorstops in iron and brass are frequently to be found.

Earlier than our period we find a gaily coloured group of Britannia, dressed in flamboyant colours, accompanied by a white lion, as rare, one imagines, as today's white tigers at Bristol Zoo. This Derby lion sports a pair of heavy black eyebrows and a purple nose and moustache. The potter Walton made a splendid lion and unicorn group intended presumably as a souvenir for the Coronation of George IV. He also made a smaller, brown lion couched by a flower-bedecked tree, all mounted on a grass-green plinth with blue twirling decorations. His figures are considered to be greatly superior to the average flat-backed ornaments and, unlike most "toy-maker's" work, his groups are often marked.

One of the most engaging ceramic lions is the one lying down with the lamb. There is a splendid Derby pair of this group, and one for the cottager's chimney, a good deal larger, made by the Staffordshire potters. Another rare Chelsea group, dated about 1760 and standing about 2 ft. 6 in. high, shows Una, in a gorgeous gold-sprigged dress with a puce lining, standing by her friendly-looking lion whose every hair is carefully modelled by the artist who created him.

It is worth remembering, perhaps, that from Elizabeth I's reign the royal lion was the figurehead of all the ships of the Navy, except those of the highest rank of "first rates", which boasted elaborate carvings of truly baroque magnificence, profusely gilded and painted, and encircling the ship round to the stern. Drawings by Van de Velde show a "first rate", *The Royal Charles*, built in 1670, which has the heraldic lion and unicorn among the massive carvings on its stern. Sample or perhaps souvenir figureheads can sometimes be found about 8 inches high. These are certainly more collectable than the full-sized figureheads, though decorative 4-ft. examples can be found giving a particularly individual character to seaside gardens.

Besides all the British lions, there are particularly beautiful ones from the East. The lion, of course, is sacred to Buddhism, and right from the Six Dynasties, sometimes called the Dark Ages of China (A.D. 220 to 589), he was used in many forms of art. The Chinese have no indigenous lions, so they made their models into extremely ferocious looking beasts, sometimes guarding a sacred tomb or defending the law.

The most unusual lions to be found in the Victoria and Albert Museum are those in a princely set of carved ivory chessmen from Bengal dated 1790. One side represents troops of the East India Company, aided by buffaloes; the other is an Indian Army aided by lions standing in the squares generally reserved for knights. The kings and queens, incidentally, are magnificently mounted on elephants.

Doorstops, paperweights and horse-brasses show the lion, while Britannia with her attendant lion appear frequently in pictures too. The charming glass pictures of the late eighteenth and early nineteenth century often show these two in the wonderfully rich colours that look so decorative on one's wall. Glass lions can also be found in Sowerby's pressed glass. These, sometimes amber-coloured, sometimes purplish black, look charming on a window-sill with the light shining through them.

The furniture-rests, which at least one expert considers to be for supporting mirrors on chimney-pieces, also show lions. Has anyone ever seen contemporary pictures of these in use, I wonder? That would solve this controversial problem.

4

A Menagerie of Ceramic Animals

The custom of keeping collections of wild animals is at least as old as history. In ancient Egypt they were appurtenances of the temples. Such well-known Biblical characters as Nebuchadnezzar and Solomon kept lions and monkeys and peacocks, while Aristotle had a fine collection of creatures brought to him by the soldiers of Alexander's army. The Romans possessed hundreds of lions, tigers and leopards of which some were kept for the grisly "sport" of killing Christians. Some of their lions and panthers were not only broken to harness but even used to retrieve rabbits. Years later Louis XIV thought nothing of spending £5,400 a year on his private menagerie at Versailles, and Augustus I had a private zoo at Dresden in 1554. Earlier in England Henry I established his Royal menagerie at Woodstock. When we visit the London Zoo how many of us reflect that it all started at Woodstock at the beginning of the twelfth century? Subsequently it was established at the Tower of London, until in 1827 the Zoological Club of the Linnean Society became the Zoo we know today and soon after united the Tower of London's collection of wild creatures with its own.

For amateur collectors animals are a very rewarding subject, and perhaps the Staffordshire potters provide the best scope, though we can also look for Welsh, Yorkshire and Scottish examples of great interest.

From the end of the seventeenth century Staffordshire proved an excellent situation for a pottery industry, with its good bed of clay to hand. Gradually the industry expanded and did so well that early in the eighteenth century John Astbury, in competition with other potters, began to produce the now famous Staffordshire figures. The early animals are those of our countryside, just as the Stone Age cave-paintings were inspired by the animals the people hunted or domesticated. The cats and dogs, the cows, the lambs and the horses, together with swans, hawks and doves and cocks of familiar everyday life are all modelled by the potters with engaging charm.

An odd thing about the animal theme is that so many creatures are left out. The pig, for instance, appears only once as far as I know, and then it has an Irish farmer on its back. This is apart from money-box pigs, of course. There aren't many owls, and few squirrels, yet these must have been numerous enough in real life. The ubiquitous lion seems an alien, sometimes lying down beside the pottery lamb, but we must remember his heraldic stature as the symbol of royalty. After all, Scots kings are said to have been invariably accompanied by a live lion until 1603.

The nineteenth century is the age of the "image toys", a title coined originally by Wedgwood; and these were also called chimney ornaments, being the poor man's answer to the splendid Meissen pieces, or the animals and birds and figures from the sophisticated factories of Bow, Chelsea, Derby and others.

The thrill of going to the Zoo became extremely popular in George IV's day, and naturally the potters were inspired to add to their vigorous, gay-coloured models some portraits of the Zoo animals which the public delighted in buying as souvenirs of their outings. The potters made zebras, leopards and elephants to increase their range. A Staffordshire tiger-hunting Rajah mounted on an elephant, of white lead-glazed earthenware painted in gay colours, is on view at the Victoria and Albert Museum, dated to the second quarter of the nineteenth century. Many animals are to be found accompanied by human figures like this Rajah. Horses are not often seen without a rider, and cows frequently have a milkmaid or herdsman in attendance. There are bull-baiting scenes which are mercifully as unreal as a fairy-story. They are also highly expensive and mostly date a bit earlier than Victoria's reign. The equestrian figures from Staffordshire are delightful, Prince Albert and Victoria, the Duke and Duchess of Cambridge, Wellington on a black charger, Dick Turpin on Black Bess, these spring to mind at once, and there are many others. *Staffordshire Portrait Figures of the Victorian Age*, by Thomas Balston, is still a collectors' standard work and well worth acquiring.

Collectors might look for the rare giraffes from Staffordshire potters. These were made in small numbers, in honour of the first giraffe to be introduced into England in 1827. It arrived as an ill-chosen gift from Mehemet Ali of Egypt to George IV and the wretched animal died for want of proper feeding.

A collection of those wittily designed cow-creamers might well appeal to some collectors, but for the beginner it is as well to study this line carefully as a number of badly designed and ugly cows are on the market. Obadiah Sherratt, the ale-house keeper and potter made a number of them. Rarely are marks to be found, but the writer owns an example, with black transfer print all over its body of a charming rural scene, and this cow has the legend under her plinth "Opaque china, Baker Beavens and Irwin". She was potted in Swansea between 1813 and 1838. Although it stretches the term Victoriana to the limit, she could be included in a collection of animals of this period perhaps. Another fine cow-creamer from the Don Pottery in Yorkshire has a very small milkmaid by her side. The honey yellow is patched with blotchy brown and pale ink-blue spots unlike any cow in real life, of course, which constitutes much of the charm of these imaginary flights of the potters' imagination. Here again is another cow rather earlier than Queen Victoria's reign.

The most likely animals to be found cheaply are the dogs of all breeds, but these and the cats and lions deserve a chapter on their own.

Rabbits, hens, goats and many birds are to be found, and if you decide that it is best to make your collection entirely from, say, Staffordshire pottery, you will find that within the range of 1837 to

1901 the simple, rather crude images, gaily coloured in strong blues and apricot and later on with less colour, all have a family resemblance. Once you've studied and carefully remembered them you'll soon become accustomed to the style. Your eye will gradually acquire the art of recognizing when your piece is "right". The potters practically never marked their work in our period, and the only way to identify pieces is by comparing textures, colours, weight and other characteristics. There is no short cut to knowledge. It is acquired through constantly handling your choice, asking dealers for help and advice and above all going to museums where the student is often permitted to handle exhibits.

A well-known dealer once told me he spent two years at the Victoria and Albert Museum, all day and every day, just looking and studying and asking questions and handling the previous exhibits, until he really felt he knew exactly what the differences were between factories and periods. His studies kept him in only two rooms, those which hold the Schreiber collection. Most of us have neither the leisure nor opportunity for such an exhaustive study, but it points the way to those of us keen to learn, and in our case a little learning is a good deal better than none. The Victorian image toys were peddled round the countryside by men and women who sold their "toys" for kitchen ornaments and the potteries made these cheaply and in large numbers so that the poorer homes as much as the well-to-do ones were cluttered with pretty pieces of decoration all over the chimney-pieces and the what-nots, the shelves hung specially for the purpose and in every conceivable nook and corner.

In middle-class homes the girls were always engaged in making things by hand, and the little image-toys were sometimes pressed into use, like one collector's little dog-kennel money-box made of cardboard and shells, which has a small Parian dog on a plinth stuck in front of the opening. The miniature models, probably made as samples for the tradesmen to take round, are another attractive idea for a collection.

There is also an enormous field for research in the fairings manufactured on the Continent and sent over to England, from about the 1850s when the Great Exhibition gave a fillip to trade, and the now well-known "go-to-bed" groups, matchbox-holders, pin-boxes and trinket boxes, many of them featuring animals. They are dealt with in the next chapter.

5

Pin-boxes and other Fairings

In the fourteenth century pins were an expensive luxury, and English law allowed them to be sold only "in open shop" during the first two days of January each year. These English pins were exported to France, which probably means that they were of excellent quality. The Duchess of Orleans ordered, at the beginning of the century, "500 long and short pins *à la façon d'Angleterre*" for her wardrobe.

One can picture how the ordinary housewives and the great ladies or their emissaries as well must have hurried off to the warehouses at the beginning of each year in order to secure for themselves as many pins as the money their husbands allowed them would buy. They kept them, most likely, carefully in little boxes just as the Victorian ladies did some five hundred years later. How fascinating it is to the collector to be able to trace the ancestry of his treasures so far into the past.

For those of us who do not despise the so-called "popular art" of the last century, there are a considerable number of different designs to look out for in these unsophisticated little boxes with figures on their lids, some of which were meant for pins, others for matches and the larger ones for trinkets. They make an enchanting collection put out all together on a table or displayed on shelves behind glass, perhaps illumined by inner lighting to show off their gay colours. In the past the great fairs used to be almost entirely markets for selling different kinds of merchandise, but by the beginning of the nineteenth century they had changed into places of amusement such as we know

Collectable Lions: *left*, the lion lies down with the lamb, a Staffordshire example; *below*, a pair of lions in lead-glazed earthenware, from Somerset

A ceramic Staffordshire cat with brilliant blue base; *below*, a Swansea cow-creamer marked Baker, Bevans and Irwin

today. There the seeker after family enjoyment that could give pleasure to old and young alike, could find any number of attractive little gifts he could buy or win at some game of skill or chance. They were very modest in price in those days, but now the pin-boxes seem to have rocketed in price and you will be lucky to find them for £5 or £6 apiece. Most of the "go-to-bed" groups, as they are now christened, and the pin-boxes, the watch-holders and the matchboxes were made by German firms, and the most prolific factory seems to have been the firm of Conta and Boehme of Possneck in Saxony, which made an enormous variety of these fairings or bazaar offerings, over a long period of time. Other factories from the Continent making similar goods were Frank Tuhten & Co. and a firm using the initials E.S.B. Keen collectors should have good reference books to consult, and a list of recommended reading appears at the back of this book.

The Conta and Boehme firm's shield containing an upraised hand is generally impressed, but Geoffrey Godden has found examples moulded in relief or overglaze printed.[1] The factory itself began as long ago as 1790 and the early examples of their groups and bazaar items were not marked. The later pieces were lighter in weight and they have "Made in Germany" printed on them often from about 1891. The "go-to-bed" groups have hundreds of different designs, and many of these are sought after as rarities. The later ones may have "Made in Japan" on them.

Of the pin-boxes there are some delightful examples like Red Riding Hood standing by the bed containing the wicked wolf dressed in Grandma's nightcap; Pretty Polly Oliver and her soldier love with his horse; kittens playing on a dressing-table; hens in a farmyard; a boy and his dog reclining on the ground; a sleeping child with her uneaten bowl of soup on the high chair. There are boxes representing fireplaces, sideboards and dressing-tables too, and a bed with a child guarded by an angel is another typical model. Less usual is a cradle with a child in a frilly cap beneath an eiderdown, decorated with

[1] *Encyclopædia of British Pottery and Porcelain Marks* by Geoffrey A. Godden (Herbert Jenkins, 1964.

roses. The distinctive dark, strong browns, dark blues, yellow-ochres and crimsons seems to be characteristic of the best boxes, and these, possibly not from Conta and Boehme, are much in demand and difficult to find.

Most of the oblong boxes were matchboxes. The roughened surfaces on the side or the inside of the lid confirm this. Other matchboxes were simply open at the top with no lids, like spillholders. There is a pair of a boy with his dog and a basket for the matches, the back of it striated for use as a striker, and a girl with a lamb feeding out of a milk churn and her basket similarly roughened as a match striker and container. These bear the Conta and Boehme shield impressed. The incised numbers sometimes found indicate the model number.

Royalty remained a popular subject and there is a charming group with a lady playing the piano while her children stand by her side singing. This is named in spidery script "God save the Queen". Boxes can be found modelled into the head and shoulders of the Queen and other well-known figures like the Duke of Wellington.

Miniature vases are an attractive subject for the small collector. They are really posy-holders. The fashion for tiny bunches of flowers was begun in William IV's reign when his wife, Queen Adelaide, who often wore a few small fresh flowers tucked into her belt, initiated a craze for miniature bouquets to decorate dressing-tables or occasional tables. Baskets or boots and shoes, even shells or cornucopias, some encrusted with tiny daisies like the ones on the pin-boxes, or with rosebuds or forget-me-nots, were very popular for many years in the mid-nineteenth century. Once more the German factories cashed in on public taste, and we see that Conta and Boehme produced vases among their huge variety of articles in "hartporzellan", or hard porcelain.

In the 1840s the factory of Copeland and Garrett introduced the now well-known Parian ware, called after the marble it resembled which was found in the island of Paros. Vases of various shapes were made in this ware and are pretty and elegant, though they, too, were

German Fairings. The boxes on the left and right with serrated edge on lids are for matches, the others for pins and trinkets. Mid-nineteenth-century and later

not expensive and there are small boxes made in this unglazed translucent white ware.

Although most of the large factories marked their work, many smaller factories did not, and there are any number of small pieces, moulded, tinted, encrusted with flowers, sometimes gilded, which are decorative and were extremely popular and therefore typical of the age we are discussing. Minton was another good firm producing Parian busts, jugs, vases and other ornaments, but these were mostly in a class above the bazaar goods with which we are concerned at present.

6

Staffordshire Figures

Anyone with a taste for Dickens would probably enjoy collecting the Staffordshire figures. The full-blooded, rollicking, humorous characters of the novelist and his unabashed sentimentality are as typical of the age as the creations of the potter.

There is a wide choice of portraits, and perhaps the beginner might start by purchasing a book on the subject, such as Louis Stanley's *Collecting Staffordshire Pottery* or the comprehensive study by Thomas Balston *Staffordshire Portrait Figures of the Victorian Age* which gives careful details of what was a lifetime's research of the subject. What suits one collector is another's poison, so suggestions as to specializing are offered at random.

The Staffordshire potters made figures of the highwaymen Dick Turpin and Tom King and of the ex-bushranger from Australia, Frank Gardiner, dressed in splendid clothes and riding on horseback. So inspired were they by these romantic villains that they made two versions of King and Turpin, unmounted and also duplicated a colourful smuggler called Will Watch, who looks particularly fine in the version wearing his sea boots and a jaunty feathered hat, patterned breeches and a striped sash. There is also a nine-inch standing figure of a baby-faced murderess called Maria Manning as well as many others infamous in their day.

Some of these figures are used twice. For example, the Frank Gardiner equestrian figure was the same model as Dick Turpin but painted differently.

There are religious subjects like "The Prodigal's Return" or featuring Samuel and Eli, and later Moody and Sankey, the American revivalists who came to England from 1872 to 1875. William Booth, who founded the Salvation Army, is another later figure but he is only shown as head and shoulders.

Actors and politicians, royalty and sport, all are there and what a picture of the period they give. Victoriana collectors might like to look for royal families. There are many of these to be found. It's important to look carefully at the modelling, for there is little satisfaction in amassing a gallery of roughly made pieces, poorly coloured. Look for the glorious, rich, ultramarine blues, rich reds and soft pinks and greens in brilliant enamel colours. But as a specialist (Anthony Oliver) pointed out in a recent article;[1] "Staffordshire" is a generic term now used very widely. He also reminds us that dealers still offer us Rockingham figures or groups which are probably Staffordshire porcelain and certainly not Rockingham unless they are marked on the base, which is simple and solid. The marks Mr Oliver tells us to look for are "the Griffin and/or ROCKINGHAM WORKS, BRAMELD, together with a mould number from 1 to 120. If the figure is very small it will only carry the mould number and possibly something which may be a gilder's mark CI 1, 2, 3, 4, etc., up to 15".

One of the fascinating things about the Staffordshire potters was the fact that mostly they worked as family concerns and were rarely influenced by foreign artists from Meissen or Sèvres. They very seldom have factory marks, sadly enough.

The French painter, the Douanier Rousseau, had the same untutored, gay, vigorous outlook as our Staffordshire potters and some of his drawings are much in the same vein—humorous, robust and full of life.

There are many figures which have elegant little patterns painted carefully on dresses and waistcoats and it is worth remembering that many of these figures were decorated by the children of the family. Since they were probably pressed into service whether talented or not

[1] *Collectors' Guide*, Aug. Sept. and Oct. 1969 issues.

it is not very surprising to find considerable variety in the quality of the work.

One piece of excellent advice to the amateur collector is offered by Anthony Oliver. He advises the beginner to go to a reputable dealer who *knows*. If you can handle pottery and porcelain in company with an expert who will give you tips on how to distinguish reproductions from originals, this is worth its weight in gold. Studying in museums, particularly if you can ask to handle the exhibit you are interested in, helps enormously too, and, of course, reading books on your subject, and checking and rechecking the facts. This is necessary in the name of accuracy, for once a mistake has been written down in print it tends to be treated as fact.

As for damage, that is a question often asked about by beginners. Probably the safest advice is to say don't take a piece where an essential part of it has been restored or is missing. The mere fact that it is not perfect will certainly affect its value if you want to sell it later on in order to replace it with something you want more. The only exceptions are rarity and great age, the last being outside our interest here as the Staffordshire figures we are discussing range roughly through the whole of the nineteenth century and a very few years into our present century.

Some of the rare figures to keep in mind are listed at the back of Thomas Balston's book,[1] and several characters were made in several patterns. Here is an example:

Grace Darling was made in a 7-in. size model with gilt script title. Here two figures are both facing to the right in the boat, Grace in the stern holding up her hands which are clasped. The man sits in the bows and to their left, on a rocky coast is a cottage, and behind them a lighthouse. The cottage has a straight roof, two windows on the first floor and a doorway. The other version differs in several respects. It is half an inch smaller, the title has gilt script as before, but Grace faces the other figure and is seated, not kneeling. The cottage roof is curved and the door has a window beside it and one central above.

[1] *Staffordshire Portrait Figures of the Victorian Age* (Faber and Faber, Ltd., 1958).

This shows that if you find two examples or even more of your subject, you need not be afraid that this necessarily means only one is original. As for the titles, these are more in demand, but not all of them are as good as many an untitled figure.

The most important part of collecting is to choose what you like. If you choose *first* for investment or prestige, you may easily falter in your judgment. Choose therefore with care and discrimination, but buy only what you really can't resist.

PLAYTHINGS OF THE PAST

1

Advertisement Dolls and Toys

In the sixteenth century craftsmen were making toys, as a side-line of their trade, out of silver and gold and alabaster. Materials as fine as this were certainly not meant for the wear and tear of the nursery; they were mainly to amuse adults who followed the craze of forming collections, which was just then becoming a fashionable pastime.

There were, of course, humbler woodcarvers, particularly on the Continent, making toys for children, and also potters making animals, whistles and toy tea-sets, as well as glass-blowers, who produced enchanting little jugs and glasses and miniature animals.

These men lived mostly in the forest areas of Europe, through which all trade passed on the rough roads. They were kept busy all the summer attending to the horse-drawn traffic but in the winter they had plenty of time to apply themselves to a hobby. So they amused themselves by fashioning toys.

Of course there were no factories then in the modern sense and before the nineteenth century the sale of toys in shops was not general. But soon the toy makers were writing out lists of prices to show travelling salesmen and by the eighteenth century the agent appears on the scene.

These middlemen soon established businesses all over Europe and catalogues, first described as "magazines", were produced towards the end of the eighteenth century.

By 1850 most specialist toy-shops were issuing these catalogues and the earliest known one, produced by a certain Mr Bestelmeier of Nuremberg, contained over 1,200 entries, boasting, in what has become customary advertising style, of his superlative toys for sale.

The nineteenth century saw a great boom in advertising. A flamboyant character calling himself "Professor" Holloway, for instance, concocted some pills and a "universal" ointment which he publicized with such success that he can fairly be classed as the very first worldwide advertiser. By 1842, four years after he had started his business, he spent £5,000 a year in singing the praises of his concoctions all over England and Europe and as far away as Peru and China. In 1843 *Punch* remarked astringently, "Mr Holloway, with the modesty which is the invariable attendant on real merit, declares that his 'universal ointment' will mend the legs of men and tables equally well and will be found an excellent article for frying fish in."

Throughout the age of Victoria it seems to have been socially acceptable for the "higher classes" to lend their names to any number of commodities. The Queen's household, as well as the impoverished Czars and other crowned heads of Europe, were advertised as using countless remedies. Another purveyor of pills enrolled no less than fifty noblemen and fifteen bishops in his register of self-styled satisfied customers.

"Sendaway offers", however, seem to have been a speciality of the twentieth century and though its origins are difficult to trace it is probable that the beautiful wax dolls, which can be seen at the Harris Museum, Preston, and were given away in exchange for tea-wrappers, were among the earliest advertisement gifts and surely the queen of this type of toy.

At the end of the eighteenth century a new paper toy "the dressing-up doll" cut out of cardboard, 8 in. high and dressed in underclothes, was invented in England. Equipped with six sets of dresses and head-dresses made out of paper, she was called "The English Doll". One hundred years later William Barbour & Sons, linen thread manufacturers from Ireland, advertised "Barbour's Dolls". These were a set of twelve dolls for three penny stamps, representing countries, period dresses and flowers including "Little Buttercup", which dates it nicely with the successes of Gilbert and Sullivan.

Among other things the Mazawattee Tea Company gave away a game of Kings and Queens, while "Force", the breakfast food, arrived on the English breakfast table from America where it had its début in 1890. "Sunny Jim" soft dolls were given away for a certain number of wrappers, "Dolly Dimple" was given away for Oxo coupons and Field's coffee offered a figure of a dandy with an eyeglass grimacing at a cup of coffee "as usually served" and beaming over a cup of Field's brew.

Pictures were frequently given away in postcard size or larger, and these in Victorian and Edwardian times were generally of personalities in the public eye or of royalties. Statuettes were handed out, pin-on badges, books and blotters.

Sir John Millais' famous *Bubbles* was, of course, bought by Pears' Soap to become an advertising feature for the firm, and other artists such as Landseer followed suit. Even the Queen lent her image to further the sale of Hudson's Dry Soap—"the Subjects' Best Friend".

There must be many of these free gifts hidden away in drawers or attics, for thank goodness there are hoarders still. A menace to their poor relatives, yet their dislike of throwing things away just in case they might come in handy one day at least has saved quite a little ephemera to amuse the social historian and throw light on customs and habits of the past which might otherwise have been forgotten.

2

Chiefly Dolls

Recently there has been a revival of interest in toys and particularly in dolls of the past. In fact it is quite difficult now to find them at a reasonable price. The early ones have long been sought after by discerning collectors and by museums. A few months ago a diligent collector was told about a Queen Anne period doll that had just appeared in an antique shop forty miles away. Alas, she arrived too late: a museum had already snapped it up. This, of course, is really a matter for rejoicing, as these most popular of toys are still to be found cherished and preserved in museums all over the country. New ones are opening devoted entirely to dolls and toys, so that at least those which have survived the years of being jumbled into nursery cupboards and played with by children whose parents have not taught them to respect beautiful things, are now on view to the general public.

Dolls go back, of course, into the earliest known civilizations, though many historians believe that the early ones were given a double rôle. First they were used for ceremonial or religious rites and secondly they were handed over to the children as playthings. The fashion doll, very much later, undoubtedly played this dual part. One was sent as an example of the best-dressed lady in France to the court of Edward II. She was the ancestor of a long line of these models, exquisitely clothed in all the elegance of the latest *toilettes*. Subsequently they were given to the children when the next ambassadress of *la mode* arrived.

English fashion dolls do not apparently come on the scene until the days of Queen Anne, but they continued to be used well into the nineteenth century. Sometimes they were made of cardboard, presumably for easier despatch, with their paper sets of dresses and hats beautifully painted by hand. The so-called "bagman's dolls" were christened by this name because itinerant salesmen carried them on horseback in their bags. In fact, the lay figures in our shop windows today are the descendants of these same "bagman's dolls".

For the amateur collector it is quite difficult to learn to distinguish between the different types of doll to be found. The eighteenth-century doll is outside our scope as collectors of Victoriana, but should you see one of these "babies", as they were called then, don't be put off by an appearance that may seem superficially unattractive. In 1969 a late eighteenth-century turned wood doll, with the usual inlaid enamel eyes with dark brown irises and no pupils and a few scanty wisps of brown hair nailed to the lightly carved head, was on sale at a well-known London saleroom. Her body and face were covered in gesso and a pale pinkish paint, her lower legs were missing and the one kid arm with its glovelike hand was pushed into the two holes in her shoulder. Originally the arms would have been fastened by a leather thong. This poor sad-looking creature, with only a much later dress to cover her bad plight, fetched £140.

On the other hand, the dolls of later periods, unless they are the lovely Jumeau fashion dolls, or those made by Bru or Décamps and a few other makes, should be in very good condition before a collector buys it at a high price. It is also important to study your subject by going to specialist museums and reading some of the excellent books by experts. John Noble, Curator of the Toy Collection of the Museum of the City of New York, has written an excellent book on the subject of dolls which is within the price-range of all of us. He has a useful section on "Hints for collectors", reminding us that there are many fakes about. He also wisely points out that quality rather than quantity gives the greatest satisfaction. Other books of value are mentioned in the Bibliography.

Mid-nineteenth-century wax doll. She is in a box which can be carried by a string through the lid

Fakes are coming mostly from the Continent, and it is the *bisque* dolls which are mostly being reproduced only too effectively. Sometimes heads don't belong to their right bodies, but in many of these cases if the heads and the bodies are old they may have been repaired a long time ago. The fakes have nylon wigs, quite unmistakably modern, and the bodies made out of a soft glove-kid are horribly white. Their bodies are badly proportioned and the clothes are usually machine-stitched.

Of course it is perfectly permissible to restore old dolls, but many of us prefer to leave them, scars and all, with their character unaltered. The trouble with re-wigging, re-dressing and touching up with paint, is that the charm and individuality is often lost. Nevertheless, wonders are often accomplished by careful and trained experts and the answer probably is that we must accept the two schools of thought. The restorers are very different from the fakers, who are unforgivable.

England introduced the baby doll about 1850, so little girls could mother and cuddle something a bit more lifelike than the women dolls from the dressmakers' establishments. Gradually the women dolls lost popularity and the men dolls became ever more scarce, except as inmates of dolls' houses; though here, too, we find a great paucity of the male sex. It is interesting to see that today the teenager doll is beginning to oust the baby from our toyshops. The psychologists no doubt will be able to tell us why.

The first talking dolls came in by about 1830, and obligingly said "Papa" and "Mama" when their arms were moved. But the "shut-eyes" were a little earlier still, the eyes opening and shutting by means of a wire pulled at the waist. A collector found one of these dolls a few months ago in working order, though the poor wax face was a network of fine cracks.

Later, as a development of the china heads, came the lead weight system, causing the eyes to shut when the doll was laid down, and this method is still in use today. It was not, by the way, until Queen Victoria's accession that blue eyes became fashionable, instead of the brown eyes customary in the doll world before this. Blue eyes have remained the most popular colour from that day to this.

The scope for collectors is so wide that it is quite difficult to decide on a special line. Some people prefer dolls' house families on account of their manageable size. Others specialize in wax dolls, hunting for the aristocrats of that type, the superb Montari beauties made by Augusta Montari, the wife of the wax modeller, between 1849 and 1886, and then later by her son, Richard Napoleon Montari. Her dolls were exhibited both at the Great Exhibition of 1851 and at the Paris Exhibition of 1855. Pierotti, another famous doll maker, came from a family believed to have been making dolls ever since the year 1100. He carried on his family's tradition by setting up shop in London in 1880.

If you prefer the wooden *deutsch* or "dutch" doll, this comes in sizes from less than one inch to over a foot high. The early dolls of this type have little prim faces painted in enamel, with very red cheeks and black hair. Dutch dolls are still being made today, so beware of those which have been splendidly dressed in period materials during the last twenty years or so. Of course, these too have their appeal but you should not have to pay the price of an antique for one.

Fashions help to date the doll and so do hairdressing styles. Some dolls have a family history to help, too. A baby doll in my collection has a piece of paper sewn on to her petticoat announcing in spidery letters, "I was bought in London in 1851."

The French Jumeau dolls, introduced about 1850, are considered to be the most lovely *bisque* dolls ever made. *Bisque* is simply an unglazed porcelain, by the way, with a matt surface. These Jumeau dolls are famous for their enormous eyes and rather spoilt beauty expressions. Some lucky ones have "paperweight" eyes, made in exactly the same way that the glassmakers used to create their sought-after Clichy or Barrarat or St Louis paperweights.

Between 1850 and 1870 the vogue for the new marble-like china called Parian inspired the doll-makers. In this material dolls usually have their features as well as their elaborately looped and coiled hair modelled and painted. China dolls were generally given black hair but those of Parian ware had light brown or golden hair.

One category of dolls to be found occasionally is the so-called "boxed doll". In the Harris Museum, Preston, there are two glazed boxes containing charming wax dolls dressed in silk and with flowers in their hair. These were given away in exchange for coupons by tea companies in the 1880s. A delightful wax doll in Jane Austen clothes was found recently in a West country antique shop. She was also in a glazed box, in a grotto of shells, with a woolly lamb by her side. Always keep your eyes open for those rare pedlar dolls with their trays of minute wares. They are sometimes in glazed boxes too. Wooden dolls, *papier-mâché* dolls, wax dolls, they are all collected by men as well as women. It is not possible in a short chapter to do more than skim the surface of this enchanting subject, which is really the history of fashion in its widest sense, for there are dolls dressed as pedlars or gardeners as well as queens and actresses.

The dolls Queen Victoria dressed were the wooden ones we have already mentioned. The early woodens of the seventeenth and eighteenth centuries were at first beautifully hand carved with articulated limbs and fine features. These were made for *crèches* and were mostly found in Catholic countries. The "Dutch" or *deutsch* ones are the sort we find today most easily, though the 1830 type is the rarer. These have painted faces and shoulders, their hands are fish-tail shaped and the hair is sometimes finished in a bun on the top or a yellow comb. They are generally called "pegwooden" dolls and were made in Bavaria and what is now called the Austrian Tyrol. Delicate grey wisps of hair painted round the face and then black over the head are characteristics of the early examples. They came in several sizes right down to half-an-inch long and these were often nestled into a walnut-shell made into a cradle by an early Victorian child or her governess. In the London Museum you will find this type of doll which was dressed so beautifully by Queen Victoria as a child, helped by her governess. She had about a hundred and thirty of them. The

Bethnal Green Museum also has a delightful collection of toys and dolls and their small belongings, while another worthwhile visit is to the Museum of Costume in Bath which has a roomful of dolls and their accessories; there are also the Kirkstall Abbey Museum, Leeds, the Museum of Childhood in Edinburgh and many others always open to the public. Here the keen collector can compare his own treasures with the national treasures which belong to us all.

(ii)

PEDLAR DOLLS

Dolls, which throughout history have served to mirror their times and give us intimate details of the clothes and customs of their day, were many of them dressed as pedlars all through the eighteenth and early nineteenth centuries.

If you have never seen a pedlar doll you really must make an excuse to go to the Victoria and Albert or Bethnal Green Museums, and there you'll find a miniature replica of the pedlars who walked the quiet hamlets and country towns of long ago.

There is an old woman in a red cloak, for instance. Her tray is weighed down with magically tiny objects from ribbons and laces to jars of pomade and song sheets. She was made about 1830. The two leather dolls at Bethnal Green, a man and a woman, are earlier, about 1790; their weathered old faces breathe out the very essence of the English countryside. The great majority of pedlar dolls were always home-made, generally in England, and date from about 1800.

What is the special fascination of these little figures? Partly the exquisite workmanship of their small wares and carefully stitched clothes, and partly the fact that we obtain a delicious peep into everyday life some hundred and fifty years ago.

Can you imagine the thrill which the traditional cry of the pedlar ringing through the quiet villages brought to the housewives and children? For they were, in fact, the earliest kind of shop. All sorts of merchandise was displayed for their customers' delight: the latest

Britannia and her Lion, a charming
example of the naïve, lively potter's
art of the nineteenth century; *below*,
boxes from the Conta Boehme factory
for keeping pins or trinkets. The cats
are especially sought after

A wax doll dressed as a Quaker. The limbs and face are of wax, the eyes of blue glass and the body of stuffed calico, *c.* 1875; *below*, antique shop for dolls in modern setting. The two dolls are German bisque, *c.* 1875

songs, the newest laces and ribbons, pots and pans, and moreover they brought the latest gossip from the big towns.

The dolls were mostly wooden though sometimes of leather. Men and young women seem to be rare. There are many old women in red cloaks and black bonnets. I was lucky enough to run to earth a charming young woman dressed very much like Queen Adelaide in bunchy sleeves and a full black velvet skirt. She has a dashing silk bonnet and wears gypsy earrings and is pretty enough to charm the money out of the hardest customer's pocket. Her goods are in a basket; the old Scots name for a basket, by the way, was "ped". She sells ribbons, needle-cases, mending silks, a doll, a parasol, a French song sheet called *Le Troubadour* and some excellent toasting forks. She also carries a packet of phosphorus matches, which a Frenchman is credited with inventing about 1790. Her date, however, must be about 1830 to judge by her clothes, and her charms are as fresh today as ever they were.

The historians say that the function of these pedlar dolls was to display the innumerable objects from the toy-shops which were catering for the popular houses of the day. They were not meant for toys. A version of the pedlar is the fortune-telling doll, with a skirt of paper leaves on each of which is a message for the gullible.

It is an interesting swing of the pendulum to find that after so many years of fashion dolls intended for the courts and nobility the pedlar dolls became popular. By contrast they show exactly how the working-class people of their day were dressed. They have a different appeal, of course, from their rich sisters, but their gay, colourful and unsophisticated charms have the vitality and engaging naïveté of our early Staffordshire pottery.

John Noble, Curator of the Toy Collection of the Museum of New York, points out that these pedlar dolls are generally under glass domes. There are also booths and stalls, forerunners of the delightful shops that can occasionally be found. Apparently two identical pedlars were found from different sources, according to Mr Noble, which suggests that they could be bought ready-made, or

D

perhaps there were patterns on the market to teach industrious children in their spare time to make these attractive dolls in the later days of Queen Victoria's reign. Here, too, we can see the faker at work. Sometimes the reproductions are simply an enjoyable pastime for talented fingers and sometimes deliberate deceptions. It cannot be too often reiterated that the innocent amateur should beware of fakes. The big salerooms now sometimes sell collections of dolls and toys and here is another splendid opportunity for the beginner to become the expert, handling the objects and noting the special points that help identification. Many dolls are marked and Gwen White's book *European and American Dolls* helps to date your treasure. The pedlar dolls of the mid-Victorian era sometimes were those made up by girls or their helpful relations, making use of the toy-shop accessories to fill the pedlar's tray. These also were carefully kept under domes and survive happily to this day. The dolls used are sometimes such lovely creatures as those made by Jumeau and by very carefully turning up the hair at the nape of the neck, or looking on the shoulders you may find a mark of the factory which made the doll.

There are pedlar dolls at most museums specializing in toys and dolls. The Tunbridge Wells Museum has some enchanting stall-holders and is among the most worthwhile museums to visit. The Rottingdean Toy Museum is another delightful place for toy-addicts to browse.

3

Houses and Shops for Dolls

Starting as a childhood toy and ending as a collection, the large dolls' mansion called "Stanbrig Eorls", which used to belong to Mrs Graham Montgomery, now delights hundreds of visitors to Edinburgh in the fascinating Museum of Childhood.

For seventy years the owner cared for this dolls' house and gradually built up the furnishings, the lighting, the water system and the family, so that it now looks much as any adult house might look after a long period of being lived in by one family of owners. Like its full-size counterpart this house has known the ravages, luckily not too serious, of a fire, and once a disastrous burst pipe caused a minor flood, but luckily no serious damage. It is now inhabited by the Bligh family of dolls. Once Mr Bligh mysteriously vanished and Mrs Bligh took a second husband. When the first spouse reappeared, having spent some years exploring the back of a drawer, she very sensibly engaged him as gardener. His splendid set of tools are displayed in a cabinet nearby; the wooden wheelbarrow, the mowing machine and the roller, the besom, the rake, the fork and spades are all in perfect scale. As for the rooms in the mansion, there surely never was such a large collection of entrancing little pieces, collected through all those seventy years and treasured so carefully. The house, like many another, has a junk room full of cast-off pieces that many of us would give a lot to own.

There is something very appealing about a miniature sized home and no wonder they are again being collected and filled with tiny period pieces. The earliest recorded house, in those days called a Baby House, is Bavarian and it was made in 1558, though it exists only on paper, so to speak, having been destroyed in a fire.

There is a splendid example of an early house in the Bethnal Green Museum. It was made in Nuremberg about 1673 and it measures 3ft. 6in. high and 3ft. wide. Filled with contemporary or near-contemporary furnishings, it gives a very good idea of how people lived in the seventeenth century.

The Dutch, of course, were the great makers of dolls' houses and indeed many historians credit them with making the very first models. They called them "cabinets" and these exquisite pieces of workmanship, mounted on stands, were filled with collectors' prizes, silver and other precious "toys" for the very wealthy and for adults to play with. These were not meant for children. Peter the Great, when he was staying in Holland, admired their celebrated "cabinets" so much that he ordered one to be made for himself. When the estimate of 20,000 guilders was exceeded, however, he decided to leave it behind. Similar beautiful houses can be seen in the Rijksmuseum, Amsterdam, and in the Hague.

For our purposes we must take a look at the Victorian dolls' houses which were at last meant not for children's education and for adults' amusement, but for children actually to play with and enjoy. Luckily Victorian children were generally taught to be very careful of their own property as well as other people's. Consequently we have a great deal of lovely miniature things still to be found by collectors today. There are mansions with grand staircases, perhaps a bit too large for average homes, but cottages with two rooms would even fit into a flat and there is a great appeal in a house within a house. Some dolls' house nurseries own a tiny dolls' house, a Noah's ark and other toys. Kitchens have a special appeal for girls and the furnishing of a dolls' room as a kitchen is an even older occupation than making a dolls' house. The first kitchens were, like the dolls' houses, educational in purpose.

A mid-Victorian kitchen doll was quickly snapped up in a country sale not long ago. At first sight she looks like an ordinary doll, but her apron opens up to reveal a kitchen full of pots and pans, dishes and tea-kettles.

One collector, the late Madame Helena Rubinstein, collected miniature rooms and among them she had an eighteenth-century dolls' kitchen together with a poultry yard attached to it, housing some china hens, ducks and turkeys all ready for the pot. There are generally cooks attached to the kitchen, but not always of the period.

Some collectors like to keep very strictly to period when furnishing their dolls' house, and this makes it a most interesting social study. Others prefer to keep all periods in their houses from the date of its supposed building. The question of dates is a vexed one as dolls' houses are not always in period themselves. The best are the family ones with history to back their claims and date them exactly. Failing this it is often possible to date them from wallpapers. Devoted collectors will strip the little walls down to the original covering and Vivien Greene, who pioneered dolls' house collecting at this present time, believes in delicate work with the fingernails. The excitement and satisfaction of finding a name and a date on a dolls' house thickly covered with modern paint is worth the effort.

Dolls' shops are another branch of dolls' house collecting and in the way that the kitchens taught children the rudiments of housekeeping, complete with their tiny meat-choppers, coffee-mills, gridirons, bellows, mortars and pestles, spoons, knives and forks, so the shops could provide education with pleasure. The scale is sometimes bigger than the dolls' houses, and Flora Jacobs, in her book *A History of Dolls' Houses*, believes dolls' shops cannot be traced back more than two hundred years. She does point out that in 1696 an inventory of toys belonging to the little Dauphin listed "nine shops of the market-place" and these were filled with shopkeepers and customers of enamel. But the Victorian period, besides the famous butchers' shops to be seen in the Bethnal Green Museum, also provided grocers' shops and milliners complete with leghorn and straw models, rolls of minuscule ribbons, lace, tulle and net for covering the bonnets and tiny feathers as well as hat-boxes for packing these miniature works of art. All sorts of shops and stalls were available to Victorian children, and some of us remember toy sweetshops of the nineteen thirties and earlier which had scales to weigh the nauseous little coloured goodies arranged on the shelves. These late shops are less desirable than the earlier ones as they are all factory made.

So for the collector who has room only for the miniature, here is the solution. The possibilities are vast. The dolls' house could be furnished as a school, an inn, a shop, a museum or an antique shop. The attraction of playing these games of imagination while accumulating valuable and beautiful pieces of past history is also enhanced by the satisfaction of teaching children, in the most enjoyable way, something about history as well as practical contemporary life.

4

Tinsel Pictures and Drama

The never-ending pleasure of forming a collection leads into many fascinating byways and the eternal romance of the theatre can be represented in many different lines. Those delightful theatrical Staffordshire figures are collected by many Victoriana addicts, and as a complement to such an interest the tinsel pictures and the toy theatre provide an excellent foil.

Samuel Pollock and his daughter started a shop selling the sheets of figures and scenes. Now their museum is a subject of pious pilgrimage for many lovers of Victoriana. The cardboard actors and actresses have the same robust and vigorous charm as the Staffordshire pottery figures. They were not intended for children originally, any more than dolls' houses and their priceless miniatures were. They were bought by people who loved the glitter and the gaiety of the stage and collected pictures of their favourite performers. Much later on we were reduced, in both senses of the word, to postcards. The tinsel pictures were sold as prints with the little pieces of gilt and silver, stars, spangles, and bright red and blue strips of paper all ready to decorate at home; or you could buy your pictures ready made-up. The early ones of Regency days are very much "popular art" and date at least as far back as Garrick.

The fashion for decorating prints with pieces of material and coloured papers was known in the eighteenth century and sometimes a collector is lucky enough to run one of these to earth; but those we are concerned with are the theatrical items of the nineteenth century. The Vincent Crummles type of acting, popular in Dickens' day, is exactly suited by the scowling villains and romantic heroes dressed in their tinsel decorations, which publishers sold with the prints for a few pence; the rosettes, swords and daggers are ready cut out in silver, and even the helmets and breastplates are included as well as a decorative feather or two and a few scraps of silk and satin. They were sold for each particular picture, some of which were big and others quite small. Landscapes and figures on horseback and the scarce ladies give a splendid appearance of sensational drama to your walls. Four figures, six and eight to a sheet were the usual sizes, besides the large ones. Then whole scenes for the backcloth and sheets of complete sets of characters for plays brought the figures into the realm of "Juvenile Drama", and very acceptable these are too. They were generally topical, including of course the ever popular pantomime and some of the characters shown were good portraits of the famous actors of the day. The fairytale palaces, the sea landscapes, the burlesque and melodrama on these tiny stages have the flavour of the fairground as well and a vitality all their own. The colours are as vivid now as ever they were, those coloured by hand, and later by stencil.

It is impossible to give more than a small taste of the variety of the tinsel pictures and the tiny stage sets. They are so popular that they have been frequently reprinted and for us the modern versions are but a pale copy of the originals. Nevertheless they give us useful clues about what we may find. Although the theatre sheets were intended to be cut out, the unused ones are extremely decorative and interesting to students of stage history. This was the period of overstatement and "ham" acting. We are so used to naturalism and cheap colour production now that it's difficult to imagine what an impact these rollicking little figures with their tiny stages and backcloths had on the children of the nineteenth century and, of course, on their elders too.

5

Money Boxes

In 1850 the Temperance Society had a drive to encourage its members to save up to buy a pig for the backyard. This laudable idea originated the name "piggy-bank".

One of the most endearing forms of money box is certainly the domestic animal. About 1790 a Yorkshire pottery made a delightful pair of cows, for example, with a farmer and his wife in charge of them. A calf stands by the wife and a spotted dog guards the farmer. The dog has those typically human arched eyebrows of the period, when the figures were so often decorated by child labour. The farmer's cow is the money box, appropriately enough. These particular spotted cows have ochre patches sponged on their bases, a characteristic said to distinguish the Yorkshire potters' work; very few money boxes are marked since they were not really meant for posterity.

The progress to wealth in primitive days was through buying beasts, so that animals were, in a way, the earliest forms of money. It suited everyone to be paid for his labour, or his craft or even his bride in cattle. Long ago to speak of a person as being impecunious simply meant he had no cattle and was consequently very poor, the Latin word *pecus*, of course, means cattle.

However, there were a great many advantages in changing from beasts to solid gold bars or, later, coins of gold or silver. These were neither subject to disease nor apt to be driven away by some villain during the night. Advancing civilization, to be sure, has certainly resulted in money being just as easy to steal as cattle, especially if it is all conveniently stored in a money box or safe. But at first it sounded a simple and easy way of exchanging goods. Aristotle declared that money had to be easy to recognize, easy to divide and easy to carry about. That seems to be a characteristic of money from that day to this. We are talking, by the way, of at least 2,000 years ago. Coins as we know them were first struck in the eighth century B.C.

Boxes in churches used to be opened on Christmas Day and the contents were called "the dole of the Christmas Box" or sometimes just "box money". This was distributed by the priest to the deserving ones of his parish on Boxing Day.

The tradition of money boxes appears to go back as far as Roman times, but they were then more often shaped like a pot than a box. The Elizabethans seem to have used them a good deal, but the collector will be lucky indeed if he finds one of these, or one of the Stuart period either. These early ones almost always must have been broken open and destroyed, the common fate of pottery money boxes. But as they were referred to rather slightingly as "an apprentices' box of earth" or "a money box of potter's clay", their loss to collectors is probably not great, aesthetically at least.

Elizabethan models were bottle-shaped, with the slot cut at a vertical angle on the wide shoulder. Experts tell us that it was not until after the middle of the seventeenth century that the slots were placed diagonally, but once again they reverted to the older horizontal position by the end of that century.

The eighteenth century also inspired a charming, tiered money box or pot which must have been designed to take different denominations of coinage. It's a wonder that so many of these humble little fabrications have survived, though no doubt they must have been treasured as ornaments and thus saved from destruction.

Luckily for us, the Victorian era is the best period to search for our quarry, and we shall find the most delightful assortment of boxes to induce thrift. The original earthenweare barrel or cone-shaped type, hand-modelled and decorated with contrasting streaks of clay slip or of runny brown and white spots, is the earliest kind of money box we are likely to find and these are eighteenth century. With tremendous luck we might possibly discover an English delft-ware example. These were first made in Lambeth in the mid-seventeenth century and the white surface is decorated in deep blue and perhaps green or purplish brown and black. If you do find one, treat it as suspect, for there are all too many reproductions: and then, if by some miracle the experts decide it is genuine, you'll be correspondingly elated.

Gradually, money box designs became so appealing that the owners must have hated to break them open to reach their nest-egg. The judiciously inserted knife, perhaps rather roughly handled, has obviously been used in some pottery slots. The eighteenth-century chickens on their high nests, surmounted by a fine hen, are often white on a chocolate-coloured ground or sometimes a reddish earthenware with a golden glaze. They were generally too much prized by their owners to be smashed open. Sometimes the hen is on her nest with a slot in her back for the coins. Sussex potteries occasionally impressed their names on speckled hens or mottled pigs, which were made there first of all in the eighteenth century and then throughout the nineteenth. Rockingham made rich brown-glazed money boxes, but that particular glaze with its curious purplish bloom, was also made elsewhere.

Thrift was a mid-nineteenth-century virtue inspired by Queen Victoria and her husband, Albert the Good. The rise of the prosperous middle-classes was built on saving. It is, then, not surprising to find these money boxes were so popular.

The variety is almost inexhaustible in pottery alone. There are cottages and beehives, cows, dogs, cats and lions, chests of drawers, hat-boxes, busts of familiar figures and some examples that can be collected in pairs, like the lions and cows. The cats and dogs very often appear as heads only, like the decapitated housewife or soldier inkpots of the nineteenth century.

There are many wooden money boxes too, in the shape of banks, some with charming Gothic windows of brass. Wooden fruit, as well as earthenware apples and pears, is not hard to find. The cast-iron and tinware boxes are most amusing, too, as they frequently have a mechanism that works at the drop of a coin. William Tell, for instance, knocks the apple off his son's head with a powerful looking cross-bow armed with a coin. The bucking mule tips off its Negro jockey so that the penny flies out of his mouth into the slot in the box on which they are stationed. The smiling Negro with his moving hand that throws a penny into his mouth is another mechanical money box, but he is much copied and not particularly captivating to most of us. A charming old man in an armchair, also made of cast-iron, is another American production and a very cosy addition to the nursery mantelpiece. Many of these toys have a registration mark to date them, which is always popular with collectors.

An eighteenth-century house with gaudy brass decorations and a 1797 cartwheel penny over its door was a particularly happy find a few years ago. The brass posts on either side of the door represent the tethering post for the horses belonging to the bank's customers. The owner of a similar money box not long ago explained that his had been made for a village boy by the local blacksmith in George III's reign. It proved to be the groundwork to the boy's fortune, for the threepenny pieces he popped into the elegant miniature Georgian bank enabled him to buy his first cow and he died a rich farmer. His descendants, still farming, have lived to tell the story of the savings bank which is now back in the hands of the family of the man who made it.

It was clearly long before the Victorian era that saving was not only customary but encouraged, for in February 1750 the time-honoured phrase "Take care of the pence and the pounds will take care of themselves" was coined by old Mr Lowndes, Secretary of the Treasury during the reigns of William and Mary, Queen Anne and George I, if we are to believe the pontifical Lord Chesterfield, who wrote a large number of letters giving good advice to his son. He adds, pertinently enough, "To this maxim, which he not only preached but practised, his two grandsons owe the very considerable fortune he left them."

Alas, there is not that incentive to thrift today. But perhaps a discerning choice of money boxes to hand down to one's grandchildren might profit them nearly as well. Let that serve for a good excuse to search for a few of these really enchanting little boxes.

6

Toys for the Victorian Child

A point about toys frequently overlooked is the fact that generally speaking they have been made by adults for other adults to buy for their children. The line cannot be drawn very easily between grownups and children in the realm of toys, for a great many objects appeal to all age-groups. Model soldiers, for instance, can be little painted wooden figures from Germany, or *papier-mâché* regiments suitable to be mown down by toy guns, or those authentic models dressed in full regalia, correct to the last button, hand-painted by Mignon.

Then there are those miniature works of art made for royal nurseries or collectors by enamellers in Limoges, craftsmen in Saint-Claude, Hamburg and Nuremberg and silversmiths in Holland. These last artists made furnishings for dolls' houses which were played with by both generations. In fact, anything adult size could be and was made doll-size.

How irresistible the magic of well-designed toys is for most of us. Even all those solemn games of instruction, the building outfits, the alphabets and multiplication tables, the jigsaws—known until the end of the nineteenth century as "dissected puzzles"—the religious toys of the seventeenth and eighteenth centuries, which were intended for Catholic children's diversion on Sabbath days, have considerable appeal for us today. There are tiny wooden altars, with accessories made out of tin, which used to be much in demand in France and elsewhere on the Continent, as well as brass chalices, holy-water sprinklers, missal-holders and crucifixes for dolls. Even musical boxes, giving out strains of holy music, were installed underneath elaborate altars. Playing at being priests and choir boys must have had just as much appeal as playing doctors and nurses or engine-drivers and shopkeepers during the week. Roman Catholic children must have enjoyed Sundays very much. As for the Protestant children, by the 1830s their Sundays kept them restricted to looking at pictures or solving jigsaw puzzles illustrating Bible stories. They could also enjoy building churches out of blocks and best of all they were allowed to play with the ever-popular Noah's Ark.

The best period for these arks is said to be between 1860 and 1870, when Noah and his family gathered as many as four hundred animals under their all-embracing roof. The favoured pairs included insects, and we find butterflies, spiders painted an innocuous battleship grey and occasionally pairs of grasshoppers and flies.

The earliest period in which a collector might expect to find an ark is the middle of the eighteenth century, though rumour has it that they were being made as early as the sixteenth or seventeenth centuries. Farmyard animals were certainly made then and of course the *crèches*, earlier still, would have had the horses and donkeys and cows in the holy stables. However, no ark has actually been documented, though suspicion rests on Thuringia, in Saxony, as a possible birthplace of the idea, because their carved dolls bear a strong family likeness to Noah and his wife and sons.

The mass-produced variety of ark made its appearance about 1800, and the early animals were very crudely carved and given only a few spots of colour. Nor did the designers worry too much about scale. The grasshopper is nearly as big as a rhinoceros, and the rhinoceros looks remarkably like a deer with an extra horn on its nose. Butterflies are as big as lions. Never mind. That may well be part of their attraction. Children have never been great sticklers for accuracy in dimensions and imagination takes care of any little discrepancies like that.

Germany has always been foremost in her skill at modelling wooden figures of men as well as animals and her folk toys are still being carved in the old tradition. Cottage workers in the past used to specialize, carving the same group of animals over and over again, thus becoming adepts at the art. There is a nineteenth-century book called "Untrodden Peaks" which describes an old German peasant who has carved cats, dogs and sheep, wolves and elephants her whole life long, to the tune of about a thousand, in two different sizes, each year. She had learnt the skill from her mother, the mother from her mother, and so the traditional craft was handed down.

Noah's arks decorated with straw-work are most attractive. Some were made by French prisoners-of-war, notably the example at Bethnal Green Museum, dated *c*. 1810 and authenticated as having been the work of prisoners at Norman Cross Prison, Huntingdon. It is just as well to mention, as we are talking about straw-work, that prisoners-of-war did not by any means have a monopoly of straw-work marquetry, as one might suppose by the enormous number of objects invariably described as their work by many dealers and collectors. The arks, by the way, are sometimes as large as 2ft. 6in. long.

Patrick Murray, curator of the fascinating Museum of Childhood in Edinburgh, reminds us that the word "toy" dates only from the sixteenth century and then included "anything from buttons to shoe-buckles or sword hilts". Now there are many museums specializing in children's toys, and others which reserve a corner for them. They are, after all, an interesting study of social history and their variety is enormous. The earlier ones were often educational in their intention. There are many collectors who specialize in one aspect of this wide field. Doll collectors, with sub-divisions for wax, china, wooden, costume or automata are now in their thousands. Men, naturally enough, tend to collect mechanical toys, perhaps the delightful balance models, counter-weighted so that they swing or twirl, never tumbling over. This idea seems to have come to Europe in the sixteenth century from the East. The simplest version is the "roly-poly", sometimes called a tumbler or "Kelly" by the Americans. It refuses to lie down.

All sorts of moving toys can be collected, from simple string-worked figures, whose origin goes back five thousand years, to the

A French dolls' house, *c.* 1885, with contemporary wallpapers and floor coverings

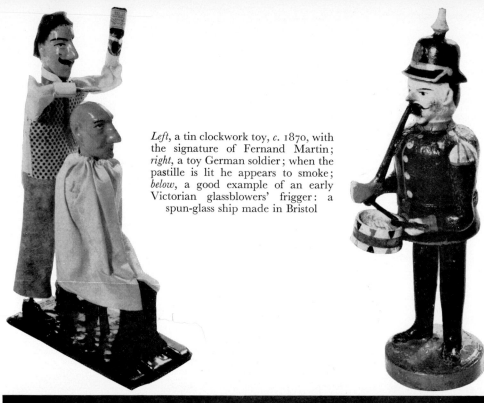

Left, a tin clockwork toy, *c.* 1870, with the signature of Fernand Martin; *right*, a toy German soldier; when the pastille is lit he appears to smoke; *below*, a good example of an early Victorian glassblowers' frigger: a spun-glass ship made in Bristol

late eighteenth-century figures weighted to tumble down ladders. A brain-child of the French toymaker was the little cardboard figure painted gaily and animated by wire, leather or string, according to its date. It is a form of marionette and is called in France a *pantin*, after a village where the inhabitants were renowned for their dancing.

The most popular toys collected by adults today are certainly the clockwork ones. Some are animated by sand or bellows or steam.

Fernand Martin is a famous name in the world of nineteenth-century clockwork toys. His lively barber endlessly polishing the bald pate of a customer with a hair-restorer, or another toy featuring a convivial fellow in a top hat trying to drink out of his bottle and to keep his balance, are both collectors' pieces now and go to show the thin line drawn between an adult's sophisticated taste and that of a child.

Here we have a few of the many toys to be found. The inventiveness of the toy-maker is a constant source of astonishment and pleasure to all ages. The little German soldier puffing at his pipe from which real smoke belches, the elegant little roundabouts fitted with doll riders and musical boxes, the realistic goat-landau driven by two fashionable French dolls, the goat rolling realistically from side to side, all these and many more can still be found by luck or perseverance today. Their price, however, is sometimes out of all proportion to their intrinsic value.

GLASS

1

Glassblowers' Friggers

A newspaper dated 1823 gives an account of a trade procession of the glassblowers, who displayed their exquisitely delicate and colourful work to the admiration of the bystanders. This particular procession carried a glass fort with glass cannons from which, believe it or not, salutes were fired. There was, moreover, a glass windmill, with moving sails and a glass bugle that really blew a martial blast, accompanied by the musical tinkle of coloured glass handbells.

These fascinating examples of the skill of the men working on glass are known as "friggers" and in Scotland "whigmeleeries", though you may not find either word in your dictionary.

They first seem to have appeared in the late eighteenth century, though bells were produced as early as the mid-seventeenth century. Handbells were originally frigged in the sense of being experimental pieces made out of the glass left over at the end of the day and perhaps sold to visitors for the price of a pint of beer. Bottle glass, out of which some of the early bells were made, was not subject to the crippling tax levied on the best quality glass. Later on it was found that bells showed off to a nicety the varieties of coloured glass, and they were therefore made commercially in emerald, red, green or opaque white glass and given knopped flint glass handles with elegant multi-coloured twists. Strictly speaking, therefore, these later, more attractive bells cannot be called friggers.

Many of the little spun and lamp-blown toys were the work of the travelling glassblowers, who carried with them their small furnaces, tallow candles and bundles of coloured glass rods. They produced any little trifle on demand, either for the merry-makers at the village fairs or for the cottagers outside their doors. They could blow a bird of paradise with a shimmering blue, white and pink spun glass tail, or a walking stick to fend off the dreaded ague, a basket, a top hat or a candlestick. The children may have clamoured for those early marbles, which are so easily distinguished from their uninspired modern counterparts by their delicate spirals of colour twists. If you are lucky you can still find tiny King Charles's spaniels encrusted with tight glass curls, and the featherweight dolls' tea-sets in opaque glass with minute flower decorations.

The Bristol Museum has a collection of charming friggers including a glass spaniel, a miniature eighteenth-century scent bottle and some fairy-like drinking glasses about an inch high, with opaque twists in their slender stems.

As always, we have to beware of imitations. These cheerful little fairground treasures have an appeal which the present-day glass-blowers can satisfy. For instance, excellent modern copies are on the market of witch-, or watch-balls, once credited with supernatural powers and sometimes intended for jug-covers to keep out dust and insects. Handbells are copied, too. The French factories make good reproductions, but the Bohemian modern copies are unlikely to deceive the expert. Remember that although glass hats and similar novelties were being made by the Americans as late as 1900, they were all far more elaborate than anything created by our own glassblowers in the early nineteenth century.

Surely the loveliest of all friggers still available to the collector is the spun glass fountain complete with bright flowers and red and blue crested birds. Another variation of it is the elegant sailing ship with delicate rigging, up which lively sailors are climbing. Sometimes an opaque glass lighthouse stands by the ship, or a smaller boat tosses on the spun glass seas. There is an example of an early nineteenth-century ship in the Victoria and Albert Museum.

2

Paperweights

In the mid-nineteenth century the English glassblowers were producing cameo paperweights of portraits of contemporary celebrities. The master of this art was Apsley Pellatt (1791–1863) and for those interested a visit to the British Museum reading room would be helpful; there you can see two of his books referring to these cameos and other work: *The Origin, Progress and Improvement of Glass Manufacture* (1821), and *Curiosities of Glass-making* (1849).

Most of the portraits were copies of coins or medals, and these were made from a mixture of china clay and super-silicate of potash poured into a mould taken from the coin or medal; after it was cooled from having been lightly baked, it was embedded in that brilliant clear flint-glass for which our glassblowers are renowned.

Sometimes the cameos were on cups of scent-bottles, basins or even decanters or later on flat plaques. A cheap type of cameo appeared at the Great Exhibition of 1851, incorporating little figures coloured in metallic paint. There were cube weights later, in 1887, commemorating the Jubilee and these were cameos of the old Queen. A firm called John Ford & Co. of Edinburgh, produced good cameos in the Pellatt tradition from about 1875.

Many different millefiore paperweights, as well as ones with birds, fruit, flowers and so on were made in England from 1845 following the example of the French, who had begun to make the exquisite examples that fetch such fantastic prices today. Our English work was not so good at first, but George Bacchus and Sons of Birmingham is a name to remember. They exhibited their "letter-weights" made in a style called Venetian star-work, which was made rather like the ancient Romans made their mosaics. These were shown at the Society of Arts in 1848 and are very rare today.

A very attractive weight, sometimes large enough to be a doorstop, is the early Nailsea flower-pot which was also made at Castleford and Birmingham. A delicious silvery pot holds a group of delicate pale-green flowers under a dome of soft green, though sometimes there are just bubbles that look like a little fountain. Experts tell us that the palest green comes from Castleford. There are also millefiore door-porters to be found if you are lucky.

Paperweights are, of course, still being made in Britain. There is a Scottish factory at Perth and an English one at Wealdstone, which used to be in London at Whitefriars. This last factory produced a paperweight to commemorate our present Queen. At the Scottish factory the weights were made by a Spanish family who settled there about 1915. These are beautifully made and not intended to deceive the unwary as anything but works of art worthy to continue the long line of successful glassmaking. The Scottish ones sometimes have PY on them and were made by the son, Paul Ysart.

Between about 1850 and 1890 interesting Victorian views for tourists were made as paperweights. These are cheap now and quite gay and colourful. After 1890, photographs were used and have little appeal for collectors.

3

Victorian Art Glass

The repeal of the Glass Act in 1845 meant that our English craftsmen could once more give full rein to their skill in the glassmen's incomparable art of manipulating our own special flint-glass, which had never been so flawlessly and brilliantly made on the Continent.

A variety of exceptionally attractive pieces for collectors can be found in Victorian glass, its most striking attribute being the many and varied colourings: there is Venetian style glass, satin glass, pearlwares in soft shaded colours, crackled, frosted, opalescent, spangled and spattered glass, purple mosaic glass ware, carnival or taffeta glass, and iridescent glass which is perhaps best known in the work of Tiffany. His first designs were stained glass, and he was that rare artist who also worked in metal, so his lamps particularly are sought after, combining as they do so successfully the two materials.

Most of this type of glass was produced from about 1850 and well into the twentieth century. American glass makers, who were inspired and helped by English designers and workers at a time when they were much in need of reorganization, seem to have been even more prolific in output than our own craftsmen. Americans, indeed, have been collecting these lovely, gay, colourful pieces much longer than ourselves.

Glasshouses at Stourbridge, Sunderland, Bristol, Newcastle and innumerable other places made what has been for years called "Bristol" glass. The French factories continue to make reproductions of milk-white glass called opaline and many other types very well indeed. Bohemian glass, too, finds its way into antique shops. Go to a reputable dealer, therefore, who will steer you past pitfalls and show you the differences between modern and old glass. But don't expect to learn in one lesson.

Burmese glass, which looks rather like a sunset, is sometimes dull, sometimes shiny and may be decorated with painting or moulded or carry applied decoration. Almost opaque, it came from America to England under the official, patented name of "Queen's Burmese". Queen Victoria ordered a tea-set and some vases after being presented with some pieces by the American maker, and consequently Burmese glass became both fashionable and expensive.

Collectors look for overlay or cased glass, which is also becoming very expensive. It has a foundation of clear glass, and then first white and afterwards various coloured casings were applied and cut out by the craftsmen, who finally polished the finished piece. Dark-blue is found most often but red, pink, turquoise and apple-green and white are also available, the loveliest of all being in a combination of three colours. Mostly this kind of glass is found in lustre-decorated vases, and the French paperweights with cased glass openings are beautiful, rare and extremely expensive.

Less rare and easy on the purse are candy-stripe glass vases and jugs. Descendants of Venetian glass, they are often basket-shaped with handles. Flowers look exquisite in these charming examples of the glassmaker's skill. Swirl bowls are very pretty too; they are ribbed often and lined and usually made of satin glass which is exactly the texture of the material and is often lined with a different colour, and also shaded. Thomas Webb of Stourbridge produced a great deal of this.

You will find moulded glass vases, jugs, bowls, match holders, scent-bottles, toilet boxes, night-light holders in many designs and made from a wide range of the art glass. Applied decoration in the form of fruit, flowers or even snakes was popular on opaline glass baskets and vases and often have pinched borders. The white and gold Bristol milk white vases are very lovely indeed, edged with a plain, clear colour, usually rose-pink.

Slagware is popular in America and we call it by this name or sometimes "agate" glass. Correctly it should be named "Mosaic glass" and one writer explains that the term "slag" is a popular misconception. She points out that it was not made out of "end-of-the-day" remains at the glassworks, nor out of coal residue.

The applied quilling on some of the art-glass, mostly the Venetian style, is an attractive decoration that looks rather like the fin of a fish. It appears a lot on the pretty cranberry glass.

The name Mary Gregory is associated with another type of yellow, green, dark-red, amber and dark-blue glass which appeared in the mid-nineteenth century. In *Victoriana* Violet Wood also helps to clear up mistakes in identifying this glass. The American glassworker Mary Gregory, who was famous for children's portraits, gave her name to this form of decoration but the original inspiration probably came from Venetian glass painted with similar figures of children. The term "Mary Gregory glass" covers all this particular style of decoration, some good and some very mediocre.

DO-IT-YOURSELF AT HOME

1

Art under Glass Shades

The 1851 Exhibition catalogue has an advertisement showing three different shaped shades "for the covering and preservation of clocks, statuettes, wax figures, alabaster and other ornaments and articles of vertu". The advertiser is the owner of a Wholesale and Retail Glass Shade Warehouse, which shows what a demand there must have been for these dust excluders. Tenniel's famous illustration of Alice kneeling on the mantelpiece preparatory to going through the looking glass shows two glass shades standing on either side of her. This was in the 1860s.

Comfort, snugness and cosiness are words especially associated with the days of Queen Victoria and comfort is surely inseparable from tidiness. The extremely crowded interiors of nineteenth-century homes would certainly have been quite chaotic without order, and the glass shades sheltered and kept in place all the innumerable fancies dreamed up by the busily leisured young woman of the period. Statuettes, clocks, stuffed birds and animals and beautifully arranged butterflies on home-made bushes were all carefully protected by the omnipresent fragile shade.

A publication called *The Young Ladies' Treasure Book* was a mine of information to help girls increase the clutter on the shelves and tables and whatnots of the average home by "various kinds of fancy work and small decorative trifles". All are eagerly snapped up by collectors today, hungry for craftsman's work instead of the mass-produced wares of the supermarkets. Thanks to the glass shades many lovely examples of what Sir James Laver so aptly calls "good bad art" have been handed down to us in excellent condition.

The delicate charms of the glassmaker's art, the fragile blown-glass birds and ships, would never have survived but for their protective shades. Many a fine automaton figure or mechanically moving scene remains in first-class condition for the same reason.

The hey-day for decorations under glass shades is probably about 1850, though the fashion goes back a good deal earlier both in England and on the Continent. One of the most exacting types of work to be covered under a shade was feather-work. Many delicate and enchanting figures and birds were made into pictures and there are splendid bouquets of flowers to be found. As making them was apparently a particularly demanding art requiring the use of a sharp knife, forceps, scissors, curling tongs and glue, together with a good pen and a painting brush, it was not as popular as the easier shellwork or arrangements of ferns, grass and seaweed and therefore does not seem to have continued long into the nineteenth century.

Shellwork and waxwork were, of course, considered to be part of every young lady's education and the shell grotto was in fashion both in the eighteenth and nineteenth centuries. A *cri de coeur* comes from a shell worker in a magazine published in 1850: "Where may shells for the construction of grottoes in gardens be purchased?" The lovely baskets of shell flowers were expensive to make and the best ones are still expensive today. In the late 1960s a shell picture of the early nineteenth century was sold at Sotheby's and was described as "a vase of flowers with painted green and blue paper leaves and the remainder in a large variety of sea shells, the vase faced with coloured stones and with white coral and contained in an ebonized and kingwood circular glazed case with a deeply moulded and parcel-gilt moulding to the front". Similar little masterpieces can be found imprisoned beneath glass shades and consequently in perfect condition. The shells were more often dyed than painted and the baskets were sometimes made of open metalwork or of more shells.

The wax-flower art was practised by many experts, who no doubt had the same tolerant contempt for the amateurs of the schoolroom and the drawing-room as the artists of any age have for the talented amateur. Well-known professional names include Mrs Strickland, Mrs Temple, who produced notably fine flowers and, of course, Mrs Peachey, who was "Artist in Wax to her Majesty".

There may have been a little jealousy among her fellow artists for her work was not very conspicuous at the Great Exhibition, where the wax-flower group occupied a prominent position but had somehow managed to relegate Mrs Peachey to a stand on private view only. Her dignified explanation is given in her book *The Royal Guide to Wax Flower Modelling*: in the original position assigned to her the sun would have melted her flowers, and when she complained it was altered to this unsuitable place. Incidentally, Mrs Peachey mentions Mary of Modena, wife of James II, as having introduced wax modelling into England, which seems surprisingly late when one remembers that the ancient Egyptians were making imitation coloured fruits and carving small figures out of beeswax to accompany them on their last journeys.

A particularly collectable group of shades is that of tinted wax groups, sometimes of birds and animals, but mostly of young people, which are carefully modelled in relief and look as if they had first been poured into moulds. The backs are always flat. They are painted and arranged, often with a background of homely trees, and have obviously been specially designed for shades. They are groups, so to speak, born under domes, while others have had domes thrust upon them.

The religious groups are generally in pale creamy wax with no additional colour, which makes them a pleasant foil to the coloured versions in a collection. These religious groups seem to have been found mostly on the Continent, though one collector found them as far away as Chile. In size they range from about nine inches to doll-size examples about two inches high. A gay little parrot in a tiny shade, a girl with a bicycle and a pair of little children dressed in the romantic revival style of Kate Greenaway's illustrations are all of them not more than three inches high. Some of the larger ones have arches of gauze dog-roses framing the figures. Many of these are about, and the smallest fit nicely into a dolls' house. In fact dolls' house shades were made and deserve mention here, although they are so difficult to find, for few collectors can resist the miniature version of his particular quarry. These tiny copies of the ubiquitous shade protect Lilliputian flower arrangements, inch-high clocks or very small Parian statuettes.

Dolls, clocks, musical figures and especially arranged groups of treasures too fragile to be left unprotected can be found dust-free and fresh under their shades. Shades alone and uninhabited cost a lot now, but that probably will not be for ever. Fashions in antiques are capricious and generally it is only things which have intrinsic value, such as silver, gold, precious stones and good furniture and pictures, which keep their value. Nevertheless, shades are very useful to collectors, protecting their precious treasures from dust and idle fingers, and certainly worth buying at a pound or two. Best, of course, to buy them protecting some lovely little piece of careful craftsmanship of a hundred or so years ago.

In a scrapbook recently there was a charming series of coloured engravings showing various trades and shops. Judging by their flat slippers, coal-scuttle bonnets and wide skirts, the lady and her daughter looking at the shops date to about 1850. In one engraving they are looking at a "chymist's" shop examining a pink jar marked "Tooth Powder" and a larger, sinister jar labelled "Leeches". In the next picture they are looking at a counter of wax flowers under tall glass domes and this engraving is called "Ornamental Industry". Mother and daughter are obviously interested in what were always referred to in the nineteenth century as "shades". To be "clever with her fingers" was the aim of every Victorian Miss. Some of the work under shades was professional, but many more took shape in the schoolroom or parlour. Luckily the Victorians in their large houses were natural hoarders, so we reap the benefit of their industry and artistic efforts today.

2

Beadwork

The Victorians designed the gayest, most attractive furnishings out of the enormous quantities of brilliantly coloured glass beads which the Venetians exported to us. Cushion covers, foot-stools, tea cosies, even complete surrounds for bed hangings can still be found. Their great advantage is that they can be cleaned with no danger of the colours running. There are chair seats decorated with beads—rather uncomfortably as it seems to our taste—face-screens, bell-pulls, mantelpiece draperies, even gentlemen's cravats. Everything that could conceivably be given a case or a box to preserve it had one painstakingly made and as often as not decorated with beads.

Most of us are attracted by gay colours, so it's not surprising that the history of beads goes back a long way into the past. Beads have been used for adornment at least since the Pharaohs, who delighted in beaded collars and armlets. In prehistoric times the first necklaces were made out of teeth or shells and bone and ivory, but in Egypt the earliest ones found by archaeologists were fashioned of stone, and later from a glazed material called steatite. Soon beads were being produced in a glorious assortment of bright colours such as blue and gold, green, amethyst and lapis lazuli. Some of the early Egyptian beads were beautifully carved in the shape of flowers and fruit.

In 3500 B.C. the most exquisite beads came from Ur, which is believed to have been the site of the most advanced bead culture of that period. They were made out of pearls, lapis, shell, faience and of etched chalcedony and cornelian. The mysteriously lovely onyx cat's eye came from Mesopotamia, about 2000 B.C. and was considered to be a talisman for preserving the eyesight.

Much later, amber beads were worn as a cure for stomach ache, and in Brittany the peasants still cherish certain beads, wearing them round their necks to ward off various ills. In fact, beads were worn in many countries and for that matter still are, more as amulets than ornaments. Superstitions associated with beads are even now very much alive. For instance, glass beads are being manufactured in the East for protection against the Evil Eye, while Iranian coracles still carry two blue beads and two cowrie shells in their rim to fend off misfortune. In Athens you may quite likely find that your Greek taxi driver has hung two blue beads by his speedometer for the safety of himself and his passengers.

In Elizabethan days beads were particularly favoured and clothes were elaborately sewn with jewels and embroidered with gold and silver thread. The ornateness of dress was largely due to the passion for finery of Henry VIII, which he passed on to his daughter Elizabeth I. At her death they counted in her wardrobe glittering bejewelled dresses by the thousand, not to mention wigs by the hundred. She bought the splendid collection of pearls which Mary Queen of Scots had acquired when she lived in France, and judging by her portraits, pearl beads were Elizabeth's pride and joy.

In France, at the same time, the covering of dresses with costly beads had become even more exaggerated. Henry IV, himself noted for his austere clothes, provided his mistress, Gabrielle d'Estrée, with a dress so heavy with pearl beads and other precious stones that the poor lady was incapable of standing upright in it without help.

It is something of a relief to come to the early nineteenth century, when, after a few ups and downs, the popularity of beads revived but did not get out of hand. This is where the collector comes into his own. Sets of jewellery were made in delicate flower designs, composed of tiny coloured beads. You can find, for example, necklaces, brooches and hair ornaments made out of beads threaded on to gossamer-fine waxed thread by means of needles of a delicacy the modern age never sees.

One of the most easily found pieces of beadwork is the purse, and more particularly the "miser's purse", which opens into a slit for the coins to be dropped in and is then kept safely in place by rings of steel or gilt. The colour and variety of these charming purses make the loveliest collection, and a good example hung on the wall beneath a picture looks most decorative. The Harris Museum at Preston has a large collection of purses and anyone lucky enough to live within motoring distance should make a point of going there, not only for the beadwork but for many other interesting sidelines of Victoriana.

By 1830 the flowery designs had superseded the geometric patterns of the Regency. The Victorians loved roses and many charming examples of these can be found. Indeed, you could make a small collection of nothing but roses or flowered beadwork. The repeal of the Glass Tax in 1845 meant that beads were cheaper, since they could be made in our own glassworks instead of being imported from Venice. Even loomed beadwork was made, which can be distinguished from the handmade work by its absolute uniformity.

Dating beads is rather a problem, but as a general guide amber, rose, turquoise-blue and green are the earliest that concern us. Crimson, dark-greens and greys date to about 1880.

In the Musée des Arts Décoratifs, in Paris, you can see examples of French beadwork. There are eighteenth-century covers for scent bottles and for scissor shields; there are handles on knives and forks made out of beads, and bead-covered boxes of all sizes and shapes. In the seventeenth century, too, they made use of beads for decoration. There were elegant book covers, watch cases and needle cases, most of them in those soft greens and golds we associate with Stuart "stump-work".

French ladies and children sent many charming gifts and souvenirs with messages in beadwork saying *Le coeur à vous*, or *Je suis sincère*, and in this delightful museum there is an enormous pipe case of pure Victorian vintage decorated in the early sky-blue beads.

A handsome flower-piece incorporating a musical box. Flowers are of muslin and the fruits *papier mâché*

An animal dish in milk glass

A selection of netted bead bags spanning nearly the whole of the nineteenth century

As we search for these exquisitely made, brightly coloured treasures, it is amusing to reflect that trade beads are still being used for sale and barter among primitive tribes today. It seems that beads, like toys, have a universal appeal.

3

Ladies' Magazines and Fashion Plates

One of the best sources to go to once the search for Victoriana becomes a study as well as a hobby is the magazine of the period. The *Englishwoman's Domestic Magazine*, founded in 1852, is only one of many such reference books. It serialized Mrs Beeton's *Household Management*.

In the volume for 1855 there is an article called "Potichomanie" in which we find that "the latest and most fashionable introduction to the ladies' work table is the art of converting plain glass vases into some quaint-looking articles as come from China and Japan; or into an imitation of the most beautiful modern vases." Sheets of coloured designs were cut out and gummed inside the plain glass vase and gummed again on top, after which a coat or two of coloured paint was added followed by a coat of varnish to preserve it. The result sounds disastrous, but it may have been attractive in 1855. Few can have survived the years, however, nor does this seem particularly sad. It only goes to show that there were many useless objects made, of small value artistically, and points the moral that collectors have to be selective.

Other articles give instructions on lace-making, beadwork, braiding, crochet, embroidery, netting and numbers of recipes, some of which are very good indeed. There is a section on "Sick-room and Nursery" which is rather startling. We find, for instance, instructions about curing "Cholera and Autumnal Complaints". But, of course, cholera was a Victorian scourge and there were several terrible outbreaks.

LES MODES PARISIENNES

A fine example of a fashion plate by François-Claudins Compte-Calix and typical of those imported by English journals in the nineteenth century

The collector will find useful articles on how to clean gold and silver lace. The instructions are very simple: "Sew the lace in a clean linen cloth, boil it in a quart of soft water and a quarter of a pound of soap and wash it in cold water. If tarnished, apply a little warm spirits of wine to the tarnished parts."

A hint on how to clean *papier-mâché* is another helpful piece of information for collectors of that delightful ware. All we have to do is to wash it with a sponge and cold water (no soap), dredge while damp with flour and then polish with a piece of flannel.

The way to bleach engravings is a little more complicated for the print has to be immersed in "oxygenated muriatic acid". This has to be obtained from a chemist and the strength of the acid can be tested by using a leaf of an old book.

An expensive, but apparently successful way of washing your silk ribbons in 1855 was to get threequarters of a pound of honey, half a pound of soft soap and a pint of whisky. Melt the whisky and soap on a hot hearth, add the honey and bottle it. Brush your ribbons with this mixture, rinse them in cold water three times and then hang out to dry. It might be cheaper to buy some new ribbons.

Besides biographies of the Bonapartes and Miss Nightingale there are stories ranging from "Miami, an Indian Legend" to "Domestic Trials" and articles on birds, costumes of the world, the employment of women, fairy tales, prize compositions, poetry and a coy monthly contribution called "Cupid's Letterbag". Florence, for instance, asks anxiously, "When a gentleman asks you, 'can he be more than a friend?' what are you to *infer*, and what would be proper to answer?" The replies are sharply commonsensical: "Alma has already behaved very indiscreetly and had better beat a rapid and decisive retreat." Or even more peremptorily, "Sarah is a wicked person."

Those interested in what is sometimes called "printed ephemera" may find copies of these magazines in bookshops. *The Gallery of Fashion* came out as early as the 1790s and so did the first issue of the popular *Ladies' Monthly Magazine*, and there are others with French titles and fashion plates which nevertheless were published in London.

The fashion plates themselves are well worth collecting and the best period is from about 1840 to 1870 when not single fashions are shown but delightful family groups of mother and daughters or friends meeting in the park or on the croquet lawn, at the seaside or sometimes watching sports or dancing in a ballroom. These delightful plates thus give us an idea of how life was lived in those days, though of course they are catering only for the upper-classes.

There are a few names to remember, for those who like to search only for the cream, but the signatures are elusive, so look hard at the corners of the plates or you may miss them. Three sisters called Héloïse Leloir, Anaïs Toudouze and Laure Noël, daughters of Alexandre Marie Colin, were some of the leading artists who specialized in fashions. Also look for F. C. Compte-Calix and Janet Lange and an apparently unidentified person who used the *nom-de-plume* of Numa.

After 1870 the magazines lost their valuable supply of fashion plates from France on account of the Franco-Prussian War. When France was on her feet again the flow started once more, but after 1900 the fashion plate degenerated into mass production and this, the end of the Victorian period, is where we lose interest in them.

4

Pastimes for Leisured Ladies

In 1851 a magazine called *The Family Friend* published a long article devoted to the arts of "modelling in cork, gutta percha, leather, paper, plaster of Paris, wax, wood etc.". Leisured ladies and the younger ones instructed by their governesses had a great deal of time to produce so patiently and painstakingly these "cities-ancient" from cork in bas-relief or "cities-modern" from cardboard.

Cork pictures can be found quite easily, and even a whole house, like a chalet with a doll of 1830 on the balcony, was discovered a year or two ago in a glazed box. This funny little piece must have been made about 1840, and behind the façade of the house trees of seaweed were stuck against a sky carefully hand-painted blue with some fleeting white clouds. An inch or two of path, bordered by cowrie shells, leads up to the front door, while a beautifully cut-out fence has two birds sitting on it and a pair of cats made out of snail-shells sit cosily by the front-door. There were many such framed scenes a little while ago, and another one, a good deal later, has a certain charm, too: this rather larger scene has a tiny house with a tennis court in front of it and inch-high "Dutch" dolls are playing a foursome. The whole thing appeared to be made out of a material resembling marzipan. Could it have been some late Victorian or Edwardian tennis-club celebration? The glass that keeps it fresh and undamaged prevents a more comprehensive study.

The Family Friend's correspondence columns were full of queries. A modeller in wax asks "Where may the glass balls required for foundations of waxen fruits be purchased at the cheapest rate?" On another page a correspondent mentions the Great Exhibition and gives a list of Waxen Flower Makers' names. There are Emma Chisholme, Jeanette Devis, Henrietta Ewart and many others, not forgetting perhaps the most famous of them all, Emma Peachey, already mentioned.

Although many shell arrangements were displayed under glass shades, a number were also designed as pictures to be framed and hung on the crowded walls of the Victorian drawing-room, and earlier on the less cluttered Georgian walls.

Another novelty was a variation of the "tinsel" picture, which consisted of dressing the figures of a print with materials and pieces of hair and jewellery and other oddments.

This light-hearted pastime was also practised in France and I have seen a pair of pictures of an actor and an actress believed to be eighteenth-century work. Two scenes of a river picnic embellished in this way, where the figures are in eighteenth-century clothes, hang in the Musée des Arts Décoratifs, in Paris. These are a variant and earlier version of the well-known "tinsel" pictures—much copied nowadays as a trap for beginners. The Prince Regent's passion for theatricals made them especially popular in his day, though in fact they were being made at least as early as Garrick. The toy-theatre sheets date back to about 1811 and the characters and scenes were on sale for what has now become a household phrase—"a penny plain; twopence coloured". The early portraits were intended for the amusement of adults, who bought their favourite artistes either already embellished or to which they added the material and tinsel themselves.

Albums are preserved in the British Museum of the work of a talented invalid, Amelia Blackburn. She invented her paper cut-outs in the 1830s, making them out of ordinary kitchen paper, fixing the pin-pricked pieces with gum and painting them. Her work was in the tradition of Mrs Delany's famous "mosaicks", an album of whose work is also in the British Museum. This delightful friend of the Duchess of Portland, herself no mean artist, was the inventor of a method of fairylike cut-outs of paper flowers. In 1774, when she invented this art, she was 74 years old. Fanny Burney describes in her diary the methods the Duchess used in her botanically faultless reproductions of flowers.

Paper cut-outs were much in fashion during the early nineteenth century and charming examples can be found quite easily. Rolled paper-work pictures, straw-work, bead-work portraits and other subjects, hair-work landscapes, skeleton-leaf pictures, shells, feathers and seaweeds made into flowers or landscapes were all used in the popular pastimes of the period. Many have their origins a great deal earlier, of course. The scope for the collector is considerable, but he needs, as always, to be selective. In all forms of collecting this is a golden rule which cannot be reiterated too often. Quality and not quantity is to be strongly urged, and the amateur collector should beware of paying too much for damaged or second-rate goods.

Painting on velvet or velours was another art of the nineteenth century. In a 1966 sales catalogue a pair of Victorian oval painted velvet pictures, described as "with sprays of summer flowers on an ivory ground in maplewood frames", fetched £34. The same catalogue listed a pair of mid-eighteenth-century Italian cut-paper and material religious pictures, which were probably made by nuns since they are known to have specialized in rolled paper-work. The pictures realized £105. However, a Victorian painting on velours of George Washington cost only £18 and another of the Prince of Wales, later Edward VII, went for £16. I have been unable to discover why velvet paintings were sometimes referred to as "theorem paintings".

Perhaps the most interesting of all these unusual mediums for pictures was the most professional one. "Marmotinto" is the impressive term for painting in sand and marble dust, which was popular for only a short time during the late eighteenth and early nineteenth centuries, though its origins go far into the past. We know comparatively little about it, except that of the few artists who tried their hand at it even fewer signed their work. George III and his son Prince Frederick were both admirers of this strange form of painting and the Duke of York possessed a fine collection which was sold after he died in 1827.

The three artists specially remembered for their sand paintings are Zobel, who came to England in 1783, a confectioner called Haas and another German named Schweikhardt. Both Haas and Zobel claimed to have invented the art, though primitive people used to make sand-patterned floors and the Japanese produced their celebrated "tray pictures" of small landscapes in coloured sand, which they had designed for many centuries. The discovery made by Haas and Zobel was a method of preserving these pictures for posterity.

Haas, who seems to have been a most accomplished "table-decker", distressed his Royal patron, George III, when he had to destroy a particularly fine decoration to a dinner table. "Haas, Haas!" cried His Majesty, "You ought to fix it!" He certainly took the King's advice, for by 1789 he had experimented so successfully in fixing sand pictures to the walls that he set about decorating a ceiling. His method was to put different coloured sands into small paper bags, such as he would have used for his confectionery icing, and sprinkle the sand through the opening in the end of the bag over a board covered with a special cement. A description of his method was given by Queen Charlotte's lady-in-waiting, Mrs Papendieck. It certainly doesn't sound an easy way to decorate a ceiling, even if the boards were made on the ground, but we cannot judge his success now as the famous ceiling was destroyed when George IV pulled down the Queen's Lodge.

Schweikhardt, who studied in Holland, used brushwork in his technique but connoisseurs consider that this spoils the effect of sand painting. Zobel, who also claimed to be the first discoverer of how to fix sand, was the most accomplished artist. He produced a great many pictures, some of which were copied from the works of other artists, including Stubbs, West and his great friend Morland, who was believed to have sometimes sketched in the outlines for Zobel to fill in with his sands and marble dust.

The poor relations of these professional pictures in sand were the small pictures made out of the many-coloured sands of the Isle of Wight from the end of the eighteenth century till fairly late in the Victorian age. They were usually about the size of a post-card and were either souvenirs or constituted parlour pastimes for young ladies. There were instructions on how to make these little pictures in many contemporary magazines. They were very simple in comparison with the masterpieces of Haas and Zobel, and they made no use of shading. In fact, the art of marmotinto was not meant for the amateur to practise, but was a serious experiment in a new medium with a matt surface which, it was thought, made it superior in some ways to oil paintings as it could be looked at from all angles.

In 1831 an exhibition in Soho Square of Mrs Dickson's pictures, which were copies of oil paintings made in what we are accustomed to call collage, was a great success. She exhibited these pictures, of which craft she is said to be the originator, at Brighton under "Royal patronage". They were more elaborately constructed than tinsel pictures, as the fabric, consisting of tailors' cuttings, was overlaid one piece on top of another so that the surface of the painting was uneven. Like Zobel she copied other artists' work, though hers were taken from Old Masters rather than contemporaries. The Victoria and Albert Museum possesses examples of her work.

Hairwork, another rather odd invention, is fairly easily found, but may well be mistaken for penwork. The hair of relatives and friends was woven into a landscape or portrait with the same mournful intention as the mourning rings of the same period. Eighteenth-century ladies were particularly adept at these sad mementoes, which usually showed a sorrowing relative standing by a large urn or mausoleum. This exacting craft must have been hard on the eyes, the fine hair lines being as delicate as cobwebs.

During the 1860s there was a vogue for decorating with ferns. You will find glasses of this period engraved with them and ceramics decorated with fern designs, and very attractive they are. There are little boxes and trays painted with ferns too. The industrious ladies with so much spare time on their clever hands embellished notebooks, needle-cases and other objects with designs of ferns, and of course the ferns grown in every conservatory in profusion and in great variety were there to be used as models very conveniently.

Shell decoration was another accomplishment which occupied our ladies of leisure, and boxes of all sizes and dimensions, some with little views on the lids, some for gloves, for ribbons or handkerchiefs and others which were for display on the parlour tables must have been made mostly by the children for gifts to enraptured parents and relatives at Christmas. There are some of these shell-boxes which I suspect were more commercial and perhaps made by cottagers for sale at seaside resorts for tourists. The early Victorian decorations, especially the beautiful shell flowers, are more sophisticated. Early in the century shells were also in favour and the Victoria and Albert Museum has a beautiful shellwork basket of elegant flowers which is late eighteenth-century work. There are museums here and abroad which show how frequently shells have been pressed into service for decoration all through history. The use of shells for artificial flowers in the nineteenth century is roughly between 1840 and 1865. They were used with paper and gauze, wool, wax or feathers. Long before Victoria's reign in 1704 shellwork was being advertised as an occupation that could be taught to children or their elders. Mrs Delany, famous for her interior decorating and varied handicrafts, was writing to her many friends about the shell grottoes and the shell flowers for nosegays she was making. She also undertook such enormous work as chimney pieces as well as the famous grottoes, and mirror frames, hanging shelves and so forth. The early Victorian shellwork about 1840 made use of tiny shells and these, incorporated into baskets and even little dolls dressed up in shell costumes, were known as "rice shellwork". Rice, in fact, was also used, together with minute beads, to clothe the pegwooden dolls. I had a charming pair of these, a girl and a boy. The sad thing about these little works of art is that they are so fragile and moult their microscopic beads, rice and shells at the slightest jolt. They are very hard to mend well.

Octagonal shell plaques in frames of rosewood, sometimes single, sometimes double, are not the work of Victorian ladies but come under the heading of sailors' Valentines (q.v.).

Besides all these arts the Victorian ladies made scrapwork screens of many different scraps. Some of them are of quite notable historic interest. For example, there is a scrapwork screen in the Carlyle Museum in London which was made by Jane Welsh Carlyle. Scrapbooks, too, are full of period charm, but often these have been fabricated recently out of a collection of old scraps.

Queen Victoria herself encouraged these artistic efforts and Prince Albert bought a picture of rare seaweeds from a lady practising screenwork, so that his children might try to produce such little masterpieces when they were staying at Osborne. Prince Albert was not the man to allow a chance for improving occupations to slip by; he liked all games to be a means of learning something useful.

These are some of the innumerable little pieces of charming homemade art to be found under our heading of pastimes for Victorian ladies.

MISCELLANEOUS SMALL TREASURES

1

Boots and Shoes

There seems no end to the odd things people like to collect, but the superstitions linked with shoes date very far back in history and for this reason, perhaps, looking for boots and shoes made from wood, glass, china, silver, pewter, brass or even slate is very popular today. Luck was associated with shoes, in the same way as it was believed that to hang up a horse-shoe brought good fortune, provided it was hung the right way up, of course, so that the ends faced upwards.

People used to believe that it brought misfortune to put on the left shoe first. Shoes are still thrown at the departing bride and bride-groom to bring them luck, and when we tie an old shoe on the bridal car, that's also for luck, though how many of us realize that the shoe is an old fertility symbol?

The history of footwear in all its infinite variety leads to any number of fascinating byways of history and that surely is one of the joys of collecting. There is a never-failing enjoyment to be had from poking about in all sorts of shops, from the finest antique dealers, who sometimes have oddments that came to them in a "lot" at a sale and which they sell off cheaply, to the junk-stall at a weekly market. The boots and shoes we collect are mostly not-for-wearing. The nineteenth-century love-tokens are the kind of thing we are after, and what a delightful variety of these there are. Glass boots and shoes were made for use as vases, wedding-cake decorations or for toasting the huntsmen. China and pottery shoes and slippers, sometimes single and sometimes joined together, are to be found doing duty as pin-cushions, stuffed with a velvet bag, or to keep pins and oddments on a Victorian dressing-table. Recently I found a tiny silver slipper obviously intended for a posy-holder in the lapel of, perhaps, a bridegroom, or his best man. A small Moorish-style slipper an inch long opened to show an assortment of gilt pins, and to judge by its ring at the back of the slipper it probably hung on a nineteenth-century châtelaine.

Needlecases were often made in the shape of slippers, sometimes silk-covered with embroidery, sometimes made of cardboard covered with beads.

Legs, with or without shoes, were favourites with tobacco addicts, either for matchboxes, like the fat metal Victorian leg, covered with leather and trimmed with silver or brass, which can be found occasionally, with the foot encased in a small, elegant little shoe with a tiny heel. Matchbox legs, by the way, were for use with the short wax vestas matches, which could be struck on the serrated sole of the foot or any other rough surface at hand. Legs and arms were made for tamping the pipe-smoker's tobacco, though sometimes they were intended for use as seals for the letter-writer, who sealed his communications with an important looking dab of wax impressed with a design or his family crest or even a love-message.

Pewter shoes were generally snuff boxes and are quite rare. The brass shoes, with a fixture to hold them upright, were probably used in the bespoke bootmaker's window to advertise the different styles he could make. There are charming *papier-mâché* shoes, ivory shoes, silver and horn ones, but the greatest variety is probably in wood. The delightful little wooden shoes with their sliding lids and brass-studded soles and "uppers" are said to have been the work of the shoemaker's apprentices at the end of their day's work. They were probably given to sweethearts or wives as presents and often have a heart or other decorations outlined in brass studs. Occasionally they bear a date. They were also intended for use as snuffboxes and the lids generally fit neatly and well. Some are dated.

The Peterborough Museum has an interesting collection of shoes: one snuff box is dated 1760 and another is a domino-box. They were both made by prisoners-of-war of the period. One collector was the lucky finder of a pair of eighteenth-century French shoes which contained over thirty tiny dominoes made of bone.

Horn snuff boxes are sometimes made in the shape of footwear, often dating earlier than the nineteenth century. There are little ones for the pocket and big, beautifully polished ones for use on the dining-table. Some of them are elaborately inlaid with bone or ivory or mother-of-pearl. Besides being used for snuff, some shoes were made as ashtrays or tea-caddies or travelling ink-wells. A recent find was a small grey shoe with laces made out of slate. This was an ink-well and a label tied on it carried a copperplate written inscription which read, "Made by the poor people of Llanberis from the slate quarries at the feet of Snowden" [sic]. Probably not more than a hundred years old, it is an interesting little piece of history and could lead to more discoveries if anyone going to Llanberis were inspired to find out something of the conditions in the Victorian slate mines.

Many elegant shoe styles are to be found in the antique shops of France, and most European countries have miniature shoes or clogs masquerading as pincushions, flasks, love-tokens, bookmarkers and other temptations for the tourists of the past.

Dating your finds should not, of course, be done entirely with reference to style. The Victorians tended to make theirs in earlier patterns. The cheaper, tourist and fairing types, are almost all nineteenth-century work, and some even early twentieth century. Wooden snuffbox shoes date from about 1800 onwards.

Sometimes Tunbridge ware boots can be found and make a happy addition to any collection.

China shoes and slippers encrusted with pretty moulded pink and white and blue flowers are usually Continental "bazaar goods". They should not be compared of course with the exquisite flower-encrusted soft paste porcelain from Bow, Chelsea and other factories in the eighteenth century and later, about 1820, copied by Worcester, Derby, Rockingham, Coalport and other of our factories in bone china. This development of bone china was introduced by Spode in the 1790s and named by Josiah Spode's son Josiah II "Stoke Porcelain". Nevertheless, the humble little shoes and vases for the poor man's market have considerable charm.

Pressed glass shoes, sometimes plain with perhaps a flat bow decorating the toe and sometimes a bright blue, and also the delightful puss-in-a-shoe ornament, were made by Sowerby's and can be found with that firm's crest mark of a peacock's head, dating to about 1876 to 1880. Another American shoe that sometimes appears in the smaller shops is a nineteenth-century trade advertisement paperweight made of iron or bronze or other materials. For instance, a very elegant boot with a frilled top and a square toe stands on an oblong plinth to advertise a shoe company.

Spirit flasks in the shape of shoes and other unexpected shapes appeared in large numbers at the beginning of the nineteenth century made of stoneware. There are other shoes made from a dark-brown treacly ware often ascribed to Rockingham, which were called "hot-water comforters" and these, says tradition, were intended to be put in a real boot, filled with hot water to warm them. It sounds a good idea; but many of these shoe flasks were never meant even to be carried in the pocket. They were simply used to advertise the spirits inside them, and naturally the corks have long since disintegrated. However, a strange-looking boot vase, resembling a white sock which has been petrified, just conceivably may have been used to warm shoes.

Before leaving boots and shoes, there is a glass boot worth searching for which was used as a stirrup-cup by huntsmen to fortify them before the chase or restore them afterwards. The jug which accompanies these amusing glasses is in the shape of a hound and the refreshing drink is poured out of its mouth; its curled tail is the handle. The boot stirrup-cup cannot be put down full, as it isn't designed to be used at table but to be handed up to the rider. Some of these boots are coloured, but usually they are in clear glass.

An unsigned fashion plate showing dresses and bonnets worn at the beginning of Victoria's reign. The costume at bottom right is for fancy dress

Pastimes for leisured ladies: *above*, this country churchyard scene, made of cork, appears to be the work of a Victorian child; *below*, a cork picture of Osborne House, Isle of Wight

Above, an early nineteenth-century velvet painting of pet dogs; *below*, two brass shoe models for display, a wooden snuffbox shoe dated 1847 and an early horn shoe snuffbox

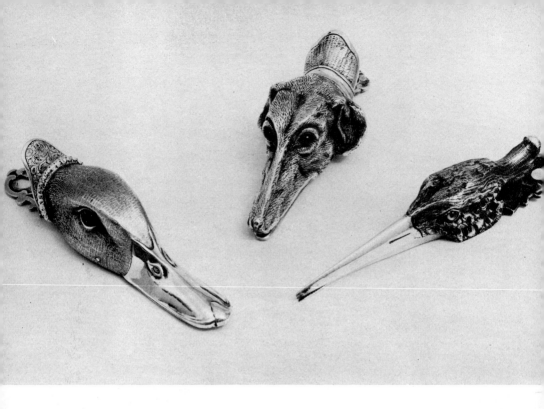

Above, heavy brass paperclips in the form of animal heads; *below*, two flower-glass paper-weights, probably Stourbridge, and a lion mask paperweight

2

Found on the Writing Table

Ideally, collecting is purely for pleasure, but we don't always have sufficient room. If you can find something small to collect there is no serious problem and one of the best fields is the many different little objects associated with the ubiquitous writing table or desk.

The history of the subject is quite an amusing source of research when you consider that the first printed book is believed to be the *Diamond Sutra*, a Chinese prayer book printed in A.D. 868. In Europe we had to wait a little longer. The first known printing press with movable type did not reach us until about 1450, and Caxton printed the first book in English in 1476.

Before this, and for that matter a long while after, all books and documents and letters to friends or on business were written by hand, and the quill was the standard pen. From the seventh century until the beginning of the nineteenth century, the quill or goose feather was used and still is to this day, for fine hand-lettering of scrolls and other manuscripts. The Romans used bronze pens. One was found at Pompeii. Roman Emperors made use of a purple ink and the quality of the unfading inks of the past was something like our present day Indian ink.

Pencils, as we know them, were produced after the discovery of a graphite mine in Cumberland in about 1600. Wooden pencils were filled with graphite or black lead. The formula has changed little since its invention. Collectable pencils in Tunbridge ware can sometimes be found.

Blotting-paper is older than you might think, since it dates back to the fifteenth century. In those days, however, it was a rarity. The early paper was so absorbent that no drying was necessary, but glazed paper, which was not discovered till the late eighteenth century, made sand or blotting-paper essential. As for indiarubber, although it did not reach us in England until the eighteenth century, it is as old as Christopher Columbus, who discovered its properties when exploring South America.

What a far cry that is from the fountain pen, invented in 1886. This surely began the decline of the inkstand and its attractive accessories with which we collectors are concerned now.

In 1759 Parson Woodforde, who was then an undergraduate at Oxford, wrote in his Diary, "Had of Mr Prince, the Bookseller in New College Lane, a standish with Sand, Ink, Wafers and half a Hundreds of Pens." Fifty or sixty years later a nineteenth-century writing table required steel nibs, at five shillings apiece at first; pen-wipers, often home-made; string-boxes; all sorts of attractive paper-clips and weights, and of course ink-stands or standishes of varying size and expense. Silver ones were complete with pounce pot and a handbell for summoning the footman who would carry the letters to their destination.

Elegant porcelain examples are numerous and also those in *papier-mâché*, sometimes with small drawers beneath the inkwells. There are odd inkwells, too, made in the shape of a head. These last were often German fairings, and you may find Napoleon, a bonneted housewife and many other odd characters made in the characteristic German hard-paste porcelain of the period. They usually have a distinctly Dickensian flavour. As with pin-boxes and matchboxes, made for the tourists or fair-goers, the mark of Conta and Boehme, with its arm holding a pointed dagger in a shield with convex sides, can sometimes be found. Remember that after 1891 the words "Made in Germany", or for that matter, any other country, will be added to the mark. This was a rule of an American Tariff Act demanding that all imported wares should bear the name of the country in which they were made.

Two Staffordshire inkwells in the Victoria and Albert Museum show amusing caricature faces. One is of Elizabeth, wife of Job Ridgway, potter of Shelton. She died in 1810. The mark is an incised N and it is dated *c.* 1810. The other is of a man and is *c.* 1840.

A beautiful Derby inkstand of about the same period, 1810–1830, is in porcelain, shaped like a basket with urns for ink inside it. The flowers are coloured in browns, purples, yellows and reds with gilding. This is, of course, a forerunner of Victoriana, but the same patterns were often repeated by factories, or brought up to date.

Another treasure in the same museum is a mid-eighteenth-century writing-box in enamel, with two glass bottles, nibs, a metal penholder and a tablet and seal.

There are beautiful examples of seals on exhibition and it cannot be too often emphasized how important it is for collectors to go to our museums and see the best examples of whatever they have decided to collect. The Victoria and Albert, so vast in its scope, is a particularly happy hunting ground for knowledge.

One of the most collectable inkpots is of iridescent glass and mounted on feet like captive soap-bubbles. Sometimes it's a rich cobalt blue but usually they are simply plain iridescent glass.

Brass paperclips are also desirable and here again you will find great variety and ingenuity. Hands, birds' heads, dogs' heads, boars' heads and other amusing shapes are to be found. These sometimes bear the diamond mark, which will date them for you exactly.

Penwipers, too, are in a diversity of shapes, from the early peg-wooden dolls dressed at home in coloured felt with decorative beads sewn on their dresses and their petticoats of muslin for cleaning pens, to the boar's head of brass with a brush on its neck for the use of your inkstained nib. A delightful little book published in 1863 gives a glimpse of what the children's lives were in that period. It is called *The Girls' Own Toymaker* and one chapter is devoted to penwipers. The butterfly penwiper is made of black velvet, buttonhole stitched all round the outside of the wings in yellow sewing silk, the inner markings chain-stitched and the wings with red silk stitching and small beads to decorate it. The witch penwiper necessitates procuring "a brown wax doll, with an old woman's face". Like the earlier peg-wooden, her petticoats serve as a penwiper. She wears, like a pedlar doll, a red cape and the instructions end "Quill up some narrow lace for a cap and make a large bonnet of black satin with a high old-fashioned crown". No pains are spared to make the old witch attractive. She is to have a small basket lined with pink calico and filled up with small pin-cushions, etc., and a small twig for a stick. That would have taken several happy days' work for the girls, and no doubt decorated Papa's writing desk very pleasingly. A doll, c. 1860, dressed as a sweep, is a good idea for a penwiper too.

Paperclips were a popular addition to any well-furnished writing table and here again there is a splendid variety for the collector. The hands of different sizes are generally in brass and not only can they be hung up beside your table to accommodate sheets of paper or outstanding bills but they generally have a diamond mark to date them. There are brass birds' heads in which the beak can clasp your letters, some very beautifully tooled and with coloured glass eyes. The greyhound will hold your papers in his brass mouth and of course there are many heavy brass, marble or glass paperweights.

These last are probably the loveliest and most sought-after writing table accessories, for the French paperweights from the factories of Baccarat, Clichy and St Louis fetch enormous prices today. The delicate flowers, fruit and millefiori patterns are irresistible to most of us, lying under their plain or faceted domes of clear translucent white glass. Even in 1963 a rare salamander weight was sold for £3,900. These factories made exquisite inkwells, too, and so did our own factories at Stourbridge, for example. These are very special writing table ornaments and deserve a book to themselves. Indeed much has been written on the subject and one should read about them as well as study them carefully before buying. They can still be found at prices less formidable than the salamander, but there are many copies. In fact, modern glass factories are producing beautiful ones fairly described as modern, and maybe some of them will be collectors' pieces of the future.

To return to our table, you might find an odd little pair of brass scissors with round ends like small coins. These are wafer-tongs, used for picking up the circular red discs used by Victorians to seal their less important letters. Documents and business letters would be sealed with wax and stamped by one of the attractive seals on a ring with or without a handle. These seals have a very long history behind them, going back at least as far as ancient Egypt. Many people collect seals in their own right and it is possible to make a most interesting collection, both valuable and beautiful to look at. You can find seals made from hardstone and sometimes mounted on a handle with several seals on a wheel, so that the writer may choose a different motto according to his mood or to suit his different correspondents. These are reputed to have been much used in France in the nineteenth century and often have both English and French devices on them. For instance, I have one with seven seals. One has *"Bonsoir"* with a candle on a blue stone; a yellow stone is engraved with a bird escaping from a cage and bears the inscription "If you neglect me you lose me"; and a compass on a black stone has *"Étourdi mais constant"* written beneath it. A word of warning, however: Don't use these seals on hard modern sealing wax or they will be ruined, as old wax was made of softer materials.

Tunbridge ware shows a most delightful assortment of useful little boxes for your desk. There are stamp boxes of different sizes, many with Queen Victoria's head when young on the lid in the form of a stamp, carefully built up from innumerable tiny squares of wood. There are rulers and letter-racks, string-boxes and blotters. The string-boxes in particular have many forms, in the way that Victorians made all their everyday objects things of charm, if not always of beauty. There are string-boxes shaped like beehives, standing on small, round feet and barrels, fruit or animal shapes as well.

Pounce pots come in a number of shapes and sizes, sometimes incorporated into the inkstand and sometimes alone in their own right. The word pounce simply means that the lid was perforated and doesn't refer to what was in the pot. The powder originally used, meant to re-surface the rough paper, was made from a concoction of gum sandarac or sometimes from powdered cuttle-fish beaks. As we have seen, the early paper was very absorbent. It was not until the end of the eighteenth century that a fine black sand was put into the pounce pot to dry the ink, for by then a glazed paper was being made.

Paper knives are also varied and attractive pieces. A Regency ram's head carved at the top of a flat piece of rosewood might have rubbed shoulders with later examples with penwork flowers curling up the length of the knife, and at the end of the century we find that the decay in writing has brought the paper knife or letter-opener to half its size. A small owl decorates the top of a little paper knife only three and a half inches long.

In the Salisbury Museum there is quite a collection of amusing writing things. A lead inkwell of the eighteenth century stands beside a notepaper box in Tunbridge ware, complete with its paper knife of the same ware, seal and pounce box. There is an early nineteenth-century quill pen-cutter and an instrument like a pair of pincers to extract rusty nibs from the penholder. Seals in their boxes are displayed, together with wafers, also in original boxes, and a braided home-made penwiper decorated with the allied flags and "Crimea 1854". There is also a usefully combined scissors and paper knife.

Nor should we forget the lovely *papier-mâché* accessories which, apart from porcelain and beautiful silver, are the most desirable of all, writing-paper boxes, blotters, pen trays and inkwells. There is a curious charm, too, in the *art nouveau* pen trays of pewter, with a high silver content. Their originality grows on a collector.

These delightful trivia of everyday life were made in all kinds of different materials. Among them there must be something for everybody.

3

Lighting the Home

The difficulty with candles was that the flame is never constant. The slightest draught and the wax spilled over the candlestick and the flame could be blown out. Even lanterns were far from easy to manage and must have been quite a hazard when everyone had bed hangings and no other lights available. Candle-guards helped, of course.

Oil-lamps, even with chimneys and globes, were not ideal, but at least the flame was more or less constant and they were generally made with heavy brass or metal bases, so that they could not overturn easily.

Collectors of different styles of illumination in the nineteenth century have the same enormous choice that this period offers in so many other collectable objects. Candlesticks alone are to be found in porcelain and pottery, in glass, pewter, wood and brass, as well as in Sheffield plate and silver.

The Victorians used an oil made of colza, carcel or rape-seed which came from the crushed seeds of kale or other brassica and was cheap and reasonably clear and smokeless. Carcel lamps date from about 1798 until late in the nineteenth century and many charmingly designed lamps used this oil. The earliest ones had no glass chimney, but the inventor, Aimé Argand of Geneva, remedied this. At first these lamps, fed by a flat woven cotton wick, were expensive to run because they used so much oil. However, this too was remedied by experiment with clockwork-driven pumps and later spring pressure.

Student lamps, with green shades to reduce the glare, were made with an original type of reservoir on the principle of the "bird fountain feed". Although these were rather cumbersome, they were, in 1830, a great improvement on previous lighting.

The duplex burner appeared in 1865 and only at the end of the century did paraffin become available on a commercial scale. The lamps with Argand burners were designed to fit neatly into pottery or china bases.

In the early 1800s the new gas lighting was tried out in some factories and in 1807 Pall Mall was triumphantly lit up with this satisfactory, if noisy illumination. By about 1840 gas lighting was used in the home quite widely, popping and singing in an alarming way, which we should certainly not tolerate today. Frosted glass globes enclosed the jets on the brass or bronze chandeliers in the 1840s. Fittings were fixed on the walls, with balloon-like shades over the gas flame. Even the kitchens boasted a chandelier. They were extremely ornate and elaborate and so were the wall lamp fixtures. They still looked rather like oil lamps, which had also been made for standing on tables and to hang or to be attached on to the wall. One comfort was that with gas there was no need to place a tray or plate beneath the lamp to collect the dripping colza oil.

Candle lamps were still in use and chamber candlesticks were kept in bedrooms. In fact, between about 1860 and 1914 there were four different ways of lighting the home. You could have candles, oil, gas or electricity. Often only the ground floor of a house was lit by gas and the rooms upstairs had to make do with candles and oil.

In the 1890s a form of light decoration which was very fashionable was a metal circle about a foot or so in diameter suspended from a central pendant from which hung silk curtains, fringed with beads or plain, according to taste. Brass, pewter, silver, china and even wood were used for candlesticks and candelabra stands, and mirror piano brackets as well.

Electric lighting had been available in the mid-nineteenth century, but for home lighting it was not in use until the carbon-filament lamp had been invented. In fact, it was not in common use until after 1914, being so costly to install. Really there was little difference in appearance between gas fittings and those for electric light in Victorian and Edwardian days.

About 1900 the American, Louis Comfort Tiffany, produced some remarkable "Pond Lily" lamps signed "Tiffany Studios". His shades were very popular, too, as were his elegant bronze candlesticks. They are in complete contrast, of course, to their late Victorian counterparts: the Victorian brass standard lamp, for example, had a yellow marble shelf half way up and a brass surround, presumably for ashtrays and matches. Tiffany and other *art nouveau* designers were in revolt against just this kind of extravaganza.

Victorian moulded or cut-glass candlesticks are the most tasteful to our standards of simpler design. Hand-painted china ones were made by Worcester and Minton and Derby and, particularly in the Minton examples, they were *en suite* with toilet-sets for the dressing-table.

There are various lamps of the late nineteenth century which were copies of the old models. Argand lamps were the earliest, being copies of the original French models, and these were made between about 1820 and 1850. They have arms sticking out carrying burners and come in sets of three for standing on the mantelpiece. The so-called Princess lamps are very pretty with the oil-well and the shade in matching glass of various colours in the different popular forms of "art glass". Sometimes the glass is cut or moulded. This is the period, between about 1820 (or in our case 1837, since we are discussing Victoriana) and the 1870s, that we find the best lamps. You will see bright blue opaque glass lamps with brass mounts which date round about 1870. The pink and white spatter glass type with a handle to carry it from room to room is another pleasing design. Sometimes a maker's mark can be found on the brass mounts.

Glass nightlights should not be forgotten in this search for illumination. Safety candles were made by Samuel Clarke of London which burnt very slowly. They had a glass or a metal base, topped with a rounded glass shade made from various elaborate forms of satin glass, Burmese, rose-coloured, striped or swirled glass. Some were enriched with pinched glass decorations. One unusual kind is the nightlight that looks a little like the shape of a lemon-squeezer. It has a stalk at the bottom enabling it to be up-ended and fixed into the top of a candlestick. It was a patented device, also made by Clarke, and the shade was clear glass shaped like a flower. The trade-mark of this and similar nightlights was very appropriately a fairy with a wand and the sentence "Clarke's patented Cricklite", while some have the words "Fairy Light" and "Pyramid" on them. These charming nightlights date from the 1860s.

The lights were used for other purposes besides comforters for children or in a dark passage. They could keep food hot, for example. The colours of the shades included all those of the rainbow and a collection of blue, red, yellow, green and turquoise shades can be extremely attractive. The only difficulty is that the metal, china or clear glass bases are often missing.

A handsome lighting for dinner-parties in early Victorian days was shown at the Great Exhibition in 1851. Designed by Archibald Cole for the Whitefriars Glass Works, the important-looking glass stand had four glass burners hung with lustres and must have looked splendid.

4

Miniature Furniture

In these days of smaller houses or flats the idea of collecting large *armoires normandes* or enormous tables, bureaux and grandfather clocks may be out of the question, but there are many miniature versions available. First, though, we must distinguish between the different categories we shall come across.

The distinction is extremely subtle between furniture meant for children's toys, for instance, and small furniture made by skilful cabinet makers in their free time or as a *tour de force*. This last can be found in nearly every style and date. Before 1790 English dolls' houses, or baby-houses as they were then called, were even designed by architects of the stature of Robert Adam, and furniture was made for them by equally professional designers, Chippendale included.

Apprentice pieces, made to test the skill of the hand and eye, are notable for brilliant craftsmanship, too, as are travellers' samples, which are extremely solid. They had to be, to stand up to a lot of handling by prospective customers. Among them you will find well-made chairs, tables, four-poster and other beds, chests of drawers, bureaux, washstands and many other charming little pieces.

It is interesting to know that as late as the 1870s the manufacturers' agents were taking round miniature samples to the retailers in preference to illustrated catalogues. One can understand why. The sales appeal of these tiny replicas must have been far greater than the humdrum illustrations.

Some of these miniature pieces were made by skilled workmen

for others to reproduce on a larger scale. In the days before scale-drawing was practised small models were often preferred by the craftsmen who had to copy them, and even after draughtsmanship became the rule, miniatures continued to be made for this reason. One point to look for is that often apprentice pieces were left unpolished, so that any defects of workmanship could not be disguised.

Moving on to toy furniture, this is now much in demand since a renewed interest in collecting dolls and dolls' houses has been born. Much of it was made at home by amateurs, and the word amateur is very appropriate to this case. The little pieces were indeed made with love and care, since so many grown-ups helped the children in Victorian days to dress their dolls, large or small, and to hem curtains or sheets and blankets, stitch rugs and tablecloths and upholster chairs and sofas, even making delightful little suites out of cork and pins covered in silk and fringed tastefully. As mentioned earlier, Queen Victoria set the vogue for dressing dolls' house inhabitants. She and her governess, Baroness Lehzen, spent many happy hours confecting elaborate dresses for the little peg-wooden German dolls now on display at the London Museum in Kensington Palace.

The early dolls' houses were made for adults first and foremost. The children might only gaze and marvel, like little Keziah in Katherine Mansfield's story. One fine lady would vie with another over the skill of her cabinet-maker, who would either make commissioned pieces of exquisite little bureaux and tallboys, sideboards, desks, mirrors, chairs and other pieces, or else some treasure from among his show pieces in his workshop might be chosen. The passion for collecting these tiny pieces went on throughout the eighteenth and nineteenth centuries, but though in the early 1800s they were still hand-made, by 1840 a large proportion of dolls' house goods came from German factories. It is these diminutive works of art, even though commercially made, that we can find most easily. There are many museums which can help us to identify our finds. Bethnal Green Museum is especially rich in these little pieces, as is the London Museum.

Fireplaces for dolls' houses, like all the rest of the furnishings, come in many different sizes. Manufacturers' samples are made out of cast-iron and have bases to stand on. The dolls' house kind cannot hold up by themselves as they were intended to be set into the chimney piece.

Look for fenders and fire-irons too, as well as coal buckets. Some of these have the diamond mark giving the exact date of their first manufacture. A good reference book of china will give details of the diamond mark on ceramics. It was used for different kinds of goods in Victorian days, between about 1842 and 1883, to register their form or pattern. From 1884 till 1909 registered designs had Rd. or Rd. No. instead of the diamond mark and the designs were numbered consecutively, giving another helping hand to those anxious to date their collection accurately. Rd. No. 550000, for example, was registered in January 1909. Remember that the diamond mark shows the earliest date of manufacture. Application to the Patent Office in London is helpful for the different classes of wares. Diamond marks appear on miniature coal scuttles, hand-paper-clips and money boxes among other Victoriana.

Jane Toller, in her *Antique Miniature Furniture*, points out that some dolls' house furniture can have a dual purpose. Chairs and stools, for instance, with stuffed seats were pincushions, and there are examples of these in the sought-after Tunbridge ware. Pincushions came in many shapes and besides chairs and stools we may find ivory or bone wheelbarrows and ivory or mother-of-pearl bellows, doll-size hats, cups and saucers, books and even fishes, which might also readily serve as a stuffed example in a glazed box on the mantelpiece. Snuff-box bellows fit well into dolls' houses, too, and yard measures appear in many charming disguises, suitable for dolls. A carved ivory basket of flowers is an example. Needlecases appeared as bellows, and bone or ivory or wood umbrellas will also fit our purpose.

Most dolls' house furniture came from Germany, but still estate carpenters and country cabinet makers produced little hand-made works of art during the early nineteenth century. The Bethnal Green Museum is the best place to go for getting the eye accustomed to "right" pieces, and the Dolls' House Museum, called The Rotunda, at Oxford, has a unique display of period houses complete with furniture for every room, including of course necessities of everyday life such as china, glass, kitchenware, books, newspapers, toys in the nurseries and lighting, heating and bathroom accessories, not forgetting all the inhabitants, dressed in period clothes. Miniature furniture of brass is very attractive and except for the nuisance of keeping it clean a collection of tables and chairs, cradles, toilet-glasses, coal buckets, candlesticks and oil lamps, trivets, kettles and grates is a delight. It has been made from the eighteenth century and tourist trade articles are still made today, so beware. The early tables are tip-up round tops with three legs, and the oval Victorian tables have heavy, turned legs and not such heavy tops. Here again, a visit to the Bethnal Green Museum will help would-be collectors.

The doll-size furniture, too big for the average dolls' house, is not so easy to display, but these pieces, some of the best being cabinet-makers' samples, or those used in shop-windows to advertise the trade, are beautifully made out of fine wood, and even dolls' house size examples can be found that show exemplary workmanship in miniature.

Chests of drawers, chairs and tables are probably the commonest pieces to find in comparison with rarities like knee-hole desks, bureaux, secretaires; and even beds and cradles are difficult to come by these days, when small articles are so eagerly snapped up. A doll-size rocking chair and another similar one in beechwood pretending to be bamboo exactly fits two late Victorian dolls. One size larger is another pair made of bentwood with plywood seats, one having "Pet" written on the back in punched holes and the other, the rocker, having "Baby" in the same place. The plywood is firmly fixed with brass buttons and these strong little chairs fit two- or three-year-old children perfectly. This type of chair was introduced in the middle of the nineteenth century. There were any number of children's pieces of furniture made in Victoria's reign, solid, well-built pieces that have stood up remarkably well to the wear and tear of nursery life.

Miniature cast-iron grates are nearly as pretty as brass ones, and sometimes they have matching fire-irons. See if you can find the tiny irons on their ornamental stands. These can be as small as an inch-and-a-half long.

Nowadays people are more aware of what they may find tucked away in an old suitcase in the loft, or lingering in that old chest-of-drawers on the landing. But a story was told to me not long ago about a small-scale tragedy involving a collection of such quarter-size chairs, rocking-chairs and other miniature treasures, which had been arranged on shelves in a house for the admiration of anyone who called there. This lovely sample furniture joined all the rubbish on a bonfire in a general clean-up and with it went a small bit of history. We are all the poorer for incidents like this. Luckily most of us collectors are natural hoarders.

Before ending our discussion of miniature furniture, one more collector's piece should be added for want of a better place to include it: look for the enchanting little miniature fiddles which were and may still be made by makers of fine violins. These are not to be found every day and don't confuse them with the *objets d'art* type made of mother-of-pearl and tortoiseshell. The ones I mean are of expert workmanship, complete replicas of full-sized violins in every respect. They were made, apparently, as practical demonstrations of skill by the experts. The famous violinist, Albert Sammons, was one of the many musicians who collected this particular type of miniature.

These wooden violins were very difficult to make, partly owing to the rarity of wood with such a diminutive grain. A well-known maker of violins himself made what is believed to be the smallest violin in the world. It is only two-and-a-half inches long.

Just as magnification tends to coarsen objects, so everyday things made in Lilliputian size have the opposite effect. They have the same attraction that a convex mirror will give to the reflection of a room. The world is seen in sharp brilliance; reality enclosed in the compass of a soap-bubble.

5

Riches on the Dressing Table

Although the use of cosmetics was frowned upon, pin trays, candle-sticks, hair brushes and hand mirrors, toilet flasks and scent bottles were all evident on the muslin flounced and beribboned dressing-table of the 1840s. Rouge, if there was any, would probably be secreted in a drawer. Glass or china vases for nosegays, flower-decorated china jugs and basins and soap dishes were *de rigeur* in the bedroom and frames containing photographs of the family began to appear. Louis-Jacques-Mandé Daguerre discovered a method of photography, its products called daguerrotypes after him, about 1840, and Fox Talbot was experimenting with his "calotype" a little later.

Bedsteads were made of brass or iron, sometimes carrying half-testers with metal rails and chintz curtains bordered with fringes, and those irresistible patchwork quilts covering the linen sheets and soft feather pillows. We find flounced muslin on the dressing tables with satin bows. The bedrooms of Victorian times were just as crowded as the rest of the house.

This is the period from which the collector can glean the ring stands and the huge silver hand-mirrors with silver-lidded cut-glass pin-boxes to match, as well as decorated combs and hair brushes, scent bottles and toilet water or sal volatile flasks, trinket trays, candlesticks made in decorated china or of brass or silver, frames in coloured enamels, wood, silver or Victorian mosaic. The catalogue of accessories is long and varied. The difficulty is not so much in finding the things as in careful discrimination.

Above, puss-in-boot late nineteenth-century inkwell; *below*, silver scent-bottle or powder-box and a walnut fitted with scent-bottle and pins, powder-box and mirror. Both late Victorian

Sailors' love tokens: *above*, a starfish pin-cushion; *below*, typical shellwork frames with nautical prints

A group of scent bottles might be a good start for a collection of accessories. Silver-capped examples come from Stourbridge in many attractive shapes and sizes and colours. Toilet water flasks or smelling bottles are most decorative and desirable in Bristol blue glass, for instance, or in honey-coloured vaseline cut-glass.

There are many beautiful little toilet boxes enriched with mother-of-pearl, and brushes and mirrors were backed by the same lovely shellwork. An enchanting glass powder bowl painted with lilies of the valley came recently into the hands of one lucky collector, probably part of a set, and china sets with that typically Victorian favourite, the moss rose or fern, can also be found with a little perseverance.

Extreme elaboration characterized the mid-Victorian dressing-table. Pin-cushions of all shapes and materials are admissible for collectors, of course, and brooches, rings, necklaces and lockets are not out of place. Ornamental scissors of this period are abundant and button hooks to do up all that multitude of buttons on boots, gaiters and gloves are also easily found. Perhaps the inclusion of a back-scratcher in the shape of a small hand with curved fingers on the end of a long stick would be stretching a point, but the very similar wig-scratcher with the straight fingers might amuse an unconventional collector.

Victorian châtelaines dating from about the 1840s are likely to have been kept if not on the dressing table at least in one of its drawers. These were worn until the 1880s and are extremely attractive; the luxurious, bejewelled gold ones with exquisite little watches attached are costly prizes, and the silver or mother-of-pearl decorated ones are charming too. Those in chased steel, though less elegant, are said to be the earliest of this period. Posy holders in silver, pinchbeck or gold were much used by Victorian ladies and surely must find a place on their dressing tables. Skirt clips were used in the 1840s, a derivation from the days when the hitching up of skirts was done by a complicated arrangement of strings and tapes. Some of them look like a pair of peculiar scissors with discs where the points of the blades should be.

One collector, without much space, concentrates on miniatures.

She has a doll-size dressing-table 8 in. wide by $4\frac{1}{2}$ in. deep and including the separate toilet-mirror it is 12 in. high. There are drawers on either side of the mirror and one across the width of the table. On it are the little accessories; a tiny brush and comb, a silver hand-mirror and a pair of microscopic scissors in the shape of a stork only an inch long. There is a scent-bottle, in cased glass, and a beadwork pin-cushion. Difficult though it is to find period pieces for dolls nowadays, this perhaps adds spice to the search. A French version of the late nineteenth century shows a posy-holder, a fan and a dressing case in this Lilliputian size. The dressing case, about the width of two average sized match-sticks, comprises brushes and combs, tooth-brush and tooth-powder, clothes brush and powder-box. This was probably part of a set belonging to one of the fabulous Jumeau dolls. A chamber candlestick, with the Derby mark on it, and a gilt fishnet purse the size of a thumbnail complete this doll's dressing table. There are nightlight holders to be found in France with a teapot warming on the top, and powder-boxes of maple wood half an inch in diameter with swansdown puffs inside.

Those interested in the history of the dressing-table and its accessories should study the evolution of the bedroom, which takes us back to the fifteenth century. Here is a quick glance into the past, which always makes the present so much more interesting.

Before the fifteenth century bedrooms were provided for only the rich man and his family and visitors. They must have been exceedingly uncomfortable by our standards, being both damp and cold, though preferable to the then average householder's sleeping arrangements where straw mattresses round the living-room fire were the best you could expect. By the middle of the fifteenth century, however, bedrooms became more cheerful, with brightly coloured plaster walls and tapestry hangings, a rug on the floor instead of rushes and a feather mattress on the carved wooden bedstead. Above the bed a canopy or tester was hung from the ceiling, and curtains to keep out the draughts were suspended on metal rails fixed to the walls. Moreover, a log fire burned in the big fireplace. But it was only in Elizabethan days that small rooms with huge beds also accommodated other furniture like chests, chairs, cupboards and toilet necessities such as a ewer and basin, cosmetic jars and boxes, and the ubiquitous chamber pot. Dressing-tables and chests of drawers and even mirrors, except for highly polished metal ones, were still to come.

By 1660 "bedchambers" were generally larger and, in well-to-do homes, besides the four-poster with its rich hangings, a table was included in the furnishings, with a dressing-box standing on it, containing drawers and a hinged and sloping mirror. The table was about the same size as the mirror and often incorporated a writing table. Sometimes the seventeenth-century dressing and writing casse were decorated with stumpwork and had a mirror in the lid and secret drawers beneath the fitted compartment for toilet and writing equipment; or the dressing boxes might be enriched with marquetry or lacquered.

Gradually bedrooms became more and more luxurious, with splendid chests of drawers, a tallboy, an elegant toilet glass, tripod washstands, bookshelves and a wig-stand. About 1750 shaving-mirrors came into fashion, mounted on a stand. Bedside or work tables were in vogue during the eighteenth century and mirrors were numerous and huge. By 1800 the feminine design of these tables with their tapering legs, small drawers and a hinged mirror, perhaps in the shape of a shield, and all richly painted and decorated, must have greatly enhanced the beautifully furnished bedrooms with their upholstery of flowered silks or stripes of delicate greens and golds. By about 1820 hanging wardrobes began to take the place of the press type and the charming little tripod washstands gave place to the large and massive washstands with mirror backs of the 1850s. Elegance began to be replaced by cosiness, which is where we came in.

6

Sailors' Love Tokens

For the very good reason that absence does not always make the heart grow fonder, sailors have been very much associated with the giving of presents to express their affection for absent wives and sweethearts. They made a great many ships-in-bottles and these lovely little pieces, said to have been made during the long night watches, date from the mid-nineteenth century up to 1914, after which sailing ships virtually ceased to be. These bottles ornamented many a cottage mantelpiece to remind the sailor of his last ship and his family of the rigours the sailors had to face in those days. The art of making them is not as difficult or slow as we might expect; the part which took longest was apparently the laying of the foundations inside the bottle, the sea and waves, perhaps a shore scene or a lighthouse. The most sought-after models are the four-masted vessels which were the iron ships called clippers.

Scrimshaw work was another occupation peculiar to sailors, a delightful gift would have been a whale tooth etched imaginatively with views, seascapes, whaling ships and other subjects. Sometimes Britannia and her lion figured on a piece of ivory or bone, or mermaids, polar bears or walruses. Hearts and messages of love, names or initials, even religious texts appear on these charmingly decorated pieces. It was the whaler, and not only British ones, either, who made these attractive presents to bring home. These long Arctic voyages gave the men a good deal of leisure, since they were often away from home for stretches of two or three years.

Ornamental stay-busks are generally late eighteenth century, some of carved wood, some of wood inlaid with ivory or perhaps bone, and some entirely of whalebone. The plain carved wood probably are not sailors' work. All of them were love-tokens and mostly they have verse or name or pictures scratched on them and stained with ink or red dye or perhaps lamp black. Knitting sticks, apple-corers and spoons may have been sailors' work too. An amusing pincushion with fishes carved on two halves of a coconut and stuffed with padding may have been bought at a foreign port, rather than being the actual work of a sailor. The early nineteenth-century shellwork plaques which Queen Mary liked so much—one is on display at the Victoria and Albert Museum—are now believed to have been bought by sailors, not made by them. Judith Coolidge Hughes, writing in *Country Life* on the subject a year or two ago, made it clear that these souvenirs, known as sailors' Valentines, with the sentimental messages of *Truly Thine*, *Forget Me Not* and so forth, were in fact made in the West Indies. The shell mosaics are made from shells common in Barbados and indeed some of the mosaics are inscribed *A Present from Barbados*. The frames are made from Spanish cedarwood and the lack of individuality also points to them being tourist pieces and not sailor-artist's work. They are nevertheless most collectable, and as their dates, according to Judith Coolidge Hughes, are from about 1800 to roughly 1880, they are certainly within the period we are discussing. They are among the most decorative and desirable of sailors' gifts.

A friend, whose seafaring husband was a Master of sailing vessels for some years and who is herself a noted collector, assured me that sailors did not make those amusing pincushions, nor the embroidered pictures of the *Victory*, celebrating Nelson's tremendous popularity and heroic death. There is, however, a striking wool picture with a hilly background and a fleet of splendid ships on a wild sea, which is said to be the work of a sailor who was hanged for murder. His sweetheart must have treasured it, since it survives to this day. Or was it *her* work of loving remembrance?

The ships in bottles, sometimes made by sailors, date from the middle of the nineteenth century, though spun-glass ships, *not* made by them, of course, were blown as far back as 1790, fully rigged and with different colours for flags and bulwarks. Often there was an opaque glass lighthouse under the dome in the background. Few of these fragile souvenirs survive intact. But they may well have been made for sailors to bring home.

Travelling glass-blowers went from fair to fair, pitching their stands and working their small furnaces for everyone to watch. The sailors, who were less agile with their fingers, or perhaps just lazy, could have chosen many of these fairings for keepsakes. The glass-blowers allowed their customers to choose what they should make for them, sometimes gossamer-fine trifles contrived from the bundles of glass rods heated by a strong tallow flame, sometimes tiny ships, sometimes a fairylike bird with a spun-glass tail, sometimes a dog or horse. In fact to this day it is possible to find small workshops where you can watch the glass-maker at work over a gas jet, giving you a glimpse of the sort of way the travelling glass-blower used to work a hundred and fifty years ago.

The coastal towns of Nailsea, Bristol, London, Newcastle and Sunderland made quantities of souvenirs and love tokens. The famous Nailsea rolling pins, with loops of opaque glass, for instance, are of a decorative type at least as old as the Pyramids. The French workmen who arrived at Nailsea at the end of the eighteenth century are said to have picked up their technique from itinerant Venetian glass-blowers. Their predecessors had learned the art from the Romans, who themselves learned from the Syrians, and so right back to the ancient Egyptians. These rollers, therefore, some of them called "Sailors' charms", have a pedigree going back more than 3,000 years.

Blue, red, green and opaque white rollers had loving verses on them, very often with a sailing ship and some such inscription as "Love and be Happy", or "The Sailor's Pride" or even "The Sailor's Tear". They were treated with great care as the breaking of these tokens was believed to herald a shipwreck. Moreover they were often filled with expensive luxuries such as tea, salt and sweetmeats; it is even said that these innocent presents were used for smuggling spirits.

Shells engraved with words like "Be true to me" or "To my dearest Mother" are still carved for the tourist in many seaside towns all over the world. The boxes covered with shells and simple shell frames round a nautical print no doubt pleased many an unsophisticated eye.

A great many jugs and basins and even wall plaques were made with an eye on the seafaring men. Sunderland ware, a generic term for several factories, was made from about 1805, and there are many delightful pieces with bubbly pink borders round pictures of ships or sailors and with appropriate rhymes. For example, what girl could resist "The Token of Jack's safe return to his True-love", with the legend beneath:

> *If you loves I, as I loves you,*
> *No pair so happy as we two.*

or again:

> *My ship is moored, my wages paid,*
> *So let me haste unto my maid.*

No wonder, as the old song has it, all the nice girls love a sailor.

7

Smokers' Toys

When two sailors were put ashore on Cuba by Christopher Columbus they observed, with no little trepidation, that the natives held in their hands "firebrands". They were speaking of the ancestor of the cigar, made out of rolled-up tobacco leaves, and the sight of the smoke issuing out of the mouth and nostrils of the Cubans must have been extremely unnerving to the two seamen.

In a very short time the news of the pleasing effects of tobacco spread to Europe and one of the ambassadors at the Portuguese court was a Frenchman called Jean Nicot, who gave his countrymen the chance of trying this new pleasure, at the same time giving the language a new word, nicotine.

Tobacco came to England towards the end of the sixteenth century and Sir Walter Raleigh is usually credited with being the first Englishman to smoke a pipe. The habit caused a great deal of annoyance to a number of people, especially James I, who wrote an angry pamphlet on the subject called "A Blast to Tobacco".

Whether the first English pipes were made of clay or silver is a matter of controversy. They were most likely to have been of silver, since at first tobacco could be afforded only by the rich. But the clay pipes with tiny bowls were the first of their kind, followed by the well-known churchwarden or alderman pipes that were made popular by William III. Clay pipes were decorated from the seventeenth century and the Victorian ones have a splendid assortment of grotesque heads. The English started to smoke cigars during the

Napoleonic wars but didn't graduate to cigarettes until the Crimean War, an idea caught from the Russians. At one period it was thought a more elegant way to take tobacco as snuff. This finely-ground powder of the tobacco leaf was introduced by Charles II and it remained a popular habit right through the eighteenth century and well into the nineteenth. Snuff-taking is as old as tobacco and, of course, by no means neglected to this day.

Collectors of smoking bygones often like to acquire Meerschaum pipes, became of their attractive carving. The word means in German literally "sea-foam", and the French call it *écume-de-mer* equally poetically. Actually, this strange material in its natural state is a form of magnesium silicate and was originally quarried mostly in Asia Minor; it is said also to be found washed up on the shores of the Black Sea. It is easily carved and the original white colouring gradually darkens with smoking.

The easiest types of Meerschaum to find are the human head, but dating is not very profitable, especially as many copies were made, and falsely dated, towards the end of the nineteenth century. They are still being made in Britain, but the imported ones from central Europe were made from the 1750s to 1860. You can find all sorts of amusing shapes besides heads. There is the typical "naughty nineties" naked lady bowl, often found in a leather case and, in fact, dating a little earlier than 1890. Ships and animals, whole scenes of hunting or war, are beautifully carved in this good-tempered material, but the simpler forms are the earliest. Generally, these have a mouthpiece of wood or ivory and later on amber is popular, for the harmonious colour-scheme it brings. You are unlikely to find a Meerschaum pipe without the mouthpiece of another material, though you may well find one with its mouthpiece missing. They are never made with mouthpieces of Meerschaum all in one, as in clay pipes. Sometimes a silver band covers the join of the two materials.

Porcelain pipes from Austria and Germany introduce a touch of luxury into a collection, if you are lucky enough to come across a Meissen or Nymphenburg head. Later on these porcelain pipes changed to the shape we know well, with the narrow, long bowl like an elongated clay pipe, attached to an elaborate stem of ivory, bone or wood or even horn. Our period produced only the brilliantly coloured paintings of girls or various scenes of the countryside and tavern. These are still being made today, but like any other antique, the old has a quality immediately recognizable once you face a new one with an old one for comparison.

Pottery pipes and even glass pipes were made in England, and though neither of them were suitable for the serious smoker they make a gay addition in colour and design to a collection.

This brings us to cigar holders, which were made in all the same materials as the pipes and would be a most rewarding collectors' quarry, for they range in subject and design quite as far as pipes. The nineteenth-century Meerschaum cigar holders, or "cigar-pipes" as they were sometimes called, were popular from the 1820s at least, when anything from a lady's leg to a jockey's cap could be carved out of this material and sometimes the most macabre pieces were incorporated into the design, such as a mouse's skull, a chicken bone or a claw. Queen Victoria's uncle, the Duke of Sussex, was an ardent collector of smokers' toys and a large number belonging to him were sold by Christie's in 1843.

Besides the pipes and holders there are many more collectors' items to be found under our heading connected with the still con-troversial habit of smoking. For collectors both with little money to spend and with well-lined purses there are tobacco boxes, tinder boxes, pipe-stoppers, cigar boxes, matchboxes and even tobacco taper sticks and miniature tongs for picking up a hot coal to light a pipe. The attractive taper candlesticks, made of solid silver and about four inches high, were for use with pipes or cigars and were never fitted with loose nozzles. They had deep, narrow sockets and were used for over a hundred years by smokers for lighting their clay pipes.

As early as the seventeenth century noblemen and royalty rubbed shoulders with the general public at the Great Fairs which had booths owned by milliners, drapers and "toy"-sellers, the last in the eighteenth-century sense of small amusing objects for adults rather than for children. Silversmiths abounded, too, and at St Bartholomew's Fair, which survived until 1855, the silversmiths specially designed their wares for gifts. They would have silver tobacco tampers, and silver corkscrews fitted with tobacco stoppers, some with animal heads. Tampers fell out of favour about 1850, but before this they were made not only in silver but in bone and ivory, pewter, wood and brass. The top or handle end was decorated with entertaining designs of animals or people. You may find a jester or a highwayman, hands and legs, animal heads and heads of Nelson or Wellington. Some of these date back as far as Charles II's restoration.

Tinder-boxes are not so easy to find, but you may be lucky and come across a brass or iron one, or better still one shaped like a pistol, which is fired by gunpowder.

Tobacco boxes are interesting, too. They are made in several different materials and you'll find wooden, china, brass, pewter and heavy lead boxes. The taverns used an amusing brass tobacco box with a slot for the coin which released a lock, allowing the customer to help himself to a good twist of tobacco, just enough for one pipeful.

In about 1870 the cigarette as we know it today was introduced from the Continent, where it had been smoked freely by the French, Spanish, Italians and Turks. There are few Victorian collectors' items connected with these, but sometimes a curious little wooden tube, a funnel with a ramrod inside it, causes a collector to pause and wonder. This is a cigarette-making machine, possibly coming from France and dating to the 1870s. The funnel was for filling with tobacco a brown paper tube, sold with this little tool in packets, and then pushed down with the accompanying ramrod. Cigarette-holders were also made out of Meerschaum, but the difference in the size of the holes quickly shows which type of smoker was being served.

Matchboxes, like tinder-boxes, essential in the collection of anyone specializing in smokers' toys, are made in many amusing shapes. A pipe was originally lit from a coal held in tongs, or from a candle or a tinder. For hundreds of years a sulphur match was used as well, this being no more than a twig or splinter of wood which had been given a small tip of sulphur at one end. The eighteenth-century matches were rather like double-ended garden labels and strung on to a wooden holder, something like a cheese board, which hung conveniently by a fire. These matches were about six inches long and both the pointed ends had been dipped in sulphur. Except to the historian these matches are not particularly collectable, but by 1828 a certain Samuel Jones of London invented a complicated portable match which came in a box comprising small tubes of acid wound round with paper soaked in a mixture of chemical, sugar and gum, which when required was broken off neatly by a pair of pliers and the paper burst into flames to light your pipe. Dangerous, one would have thought, and expensive since each tube was expendable, but the idea of portable matches was there. It was, in fact, another man called John Walker who, a year earlier, had produced "Friction Lights" which were ancestors of our present-day book-matches.

Not to be outdone, Samuel Jones produced a special match for smokers, called a Fuzee, in 1832. This was a great success, as it smouldered and was torn off in the same way as the "Friction Lights" and was still being marketed in 1860, by which time it was delicately scented. After this came another type called Vesuvius, with an enormous head ignited against any rough surface, but it was very dangerous as its stem burnt off long before the head had finished smouldering, with consequent danger to any burnable clothing or carpets. Lucifers and Congreves and then wax-stemmed Swan vestas appeared on the scene and since they were all much too dangerous to carry loose in the pockets, from about 1830 until safety matches were invented in 1855, an enormous number of enchanting boxes were made in which matches could safely be carried. They went on being made long after safety matches appeared, of course.

Here the collector comes into his own and looks delightedly for these amusing boxes, all with a roughened surface somewhere about them to show their use. Metal was a favourite material and here you find boots, shoes, arms and legs, claws of crabs and fishes, Punch, several kinds of owls and other birds, dogs' heads, barrels, crowns, letter boxes and even a cat on its stool playing a piano. Some are for hanging on a gentleman's chain across his waistcoat, with his gold watch and seals, while others are for use on the writing desk. Then there are the china fairing types, which in themselves make a charming collection. Generally foreign, they were made in quantities by Conta and Boehme of Possneck in Saxony and appeared at bazaars and fairs from the Great Exhibition in 1851. Again, look for the grooves either under the lid or hidden on a child's basket, or the back of an animal, which gives you proof of the box having been designed as a match-holder. The different figures make a varied collection, some being prettier and less crude than others, and there are examples probably intended for the French market. The factories produced all sorts of "bazaar" goods for their ever-growing market abroad.

8

Some Chairs to Collect

Chairs have not always been as comfortable as they were in Victorian days. Until about 1700 there was little difference between a chair and a stool. Painted chairs, *papier-mâché*, japanned beechwood, basketwork, bentwood rocking chairs, all can be found in the Victorian era. A birch chair with its rush seat, dated between 1880–85, is comfortable, elegant and light to carry from one room to another. Mahogany corner chairs with leather seats and rather Gothic looking backs were popular in the 1880s, and squeaky basket chairs with chintz-covered cushions were much favoured at the same period. They originated way back in the third century, forerunners of our garden chairs. Cast-iron garden chairs were popular, too, and some of these, as well as the elaborately decorated garden seats in cast-iron, are fetching high prices today. They often have charming cabriole legs and look delightful in a garden. In fact their interest to us is more in their decorative value and, of course, period flavour than their comfort. They have rounded scrolled backs and sometimes only three legs. Hall chairs were also made of cast-iron during the middle of the nineteenth century. Chippendale's design for a metal garden chair to be placed in a grotto is all scrolled shells and dolphin legs and looks indescribably uncomfortable.

The rocking chair was extremely popular a few years ago, but seems to have gone out of favour again. The bentwood and cane variety was in full swing, so to speak, in the 1860s and continued in favour until at least the 1880s.

The Great Exhibition saw the advent of the double-chair, with a useful little table-rest in between, and the "companion chair" with three conjoined seats. Its relation, the ottoman, originated in the Regency period and became a centrepiece of the room in about 1850; it was designed with a back in the middle so that people could sit all round it, and a potted palm might inconveniently be perched on the centre of it for good value. A similar chair, popular in France in the 1870s, was called the *"confidante"*. This, however, is getting nearer to the sofa or settee than the chair.

Early Victorian *papier-mâché* chairs are very desirable, and so are those charmingly curved chairs with upholstered seats and backs made of carved walnut, dating to about 1855. Rococo-style mahogany chairs, also upholstered, date to the same period and a few years later.

An oddity of the late nineteenth century was the divan easy chair. It was an armchair which had a very long seat shaped in a half-moon and projecting beyond the arms so that it would accommodate a pair of weary legs of pretty well any length. The backs of these chairs were usually buttoned and in common with most Victorian inventions for the home were very cosy. Presumably they were inspired by the "duchesse" which Hepplewhite's *Guide* (1788) advertised. This piece of furniture was composed of three parts—two armchairs and a stool which joined together into an elegant sort of day-bed if required.

The so-called lounge or lounging chair, with its long seat and bobbin-turned, barley-sugar woodwork is rather ungainly but comfortable. The Victorians used a great variety of woods, including rosewood and ebony, satinwood, walnut, some mahogany and the detestable "fumed oak". When we reach William Morris and his revival of the cottage work of the fifteenth and sixteenth centuries we find craftsmen's work and old woods being used such as elm, yew and oak. It is probably safe to say that by 1900 practically all furniture was being copied from Jacobean, Stuart or eighteenth-century designs, so that the originality of such men as first Morris and then Gimson and Barnsley was quite a novelty. Art Nouveau chairs, made about 1899, show long backs with short legs and often

127

cane seats; certainly they are original in design, though how comfortable they are is another matter.

There is one point that has to be laboured yet again. Chairs, like other furniture, are faked. That is, they are made up in some cases, or repaired, and if you are looking at an armchair, particularly the "carver" in a set, it may well have new arms added. This only means your chair should cost less, not that it isn't at least partly genuine. Many other examples of how to spot fakes can be found in good books on furniture. Suffice it to remind us that, as one well-known collector has said, "the established dealer with a high reputation is a friend of the collector." So look for a dealer of integrity. One consolation for the higher price you will pay than for what you may pick up elsewhere is that your acquisition will almost certainly increase in value with the passing years.

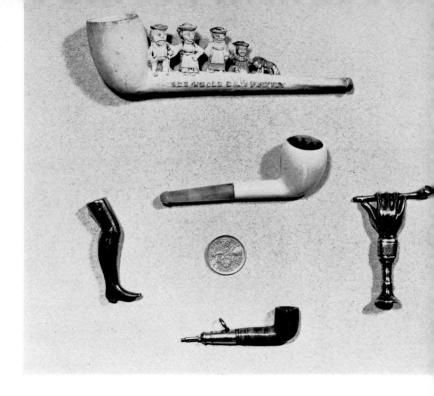

Above, selection of Victorian pipes and tampers; *below*, two remarkably well-made items
of miniature furniture from France, *c.* 1880

Beadwork chair with Berlin wool embroidery, *c.* 1850; *below*, Art Nouveau picture frames: the two small frames are of silver with peacock-coloured enamel and the large frame of plain silver

9

Art Nouveau

Although Art Nouveau had its roots in Victorian days, appearing early in the 1880s, its influence reaches far into the twentieth century. Victoriana lovers may instinctively recoil from this strange, imaginative, completely new form of art which repels and fascinates in almost equal doses. It seems to embody the clash between two conflicting ideals. Some will see it only as degenerate—"that strange decorative disease", as Walter Crane called it, while practising it himself in his wallpaper designs and book illustrations. Others find in it a new form of beauty and an expression of the machine-age translated into art. Art Nouveau is a restless, imaginative, revolutionary anti-style movement which is original, unique and, as they were never tired of saying, new.

The producers of fine arts in the first half of the nineteenth century were obsessed by nature. They copied it more or less slavishly just as our artists have always copied past styles. Look at our Renaissance and Gothic architecture. The Art Nouveau followers never did this. They were inspired by Rococo art or by Spanish, Turkish, Moorish and Oriental decorative works and by Celtic and Tudor furniture designs, but they never imitated the sources of their inspiration. Their art was indeed new. They looked at Oriental art or Japanese prints and furniture, for example, and then produced one of their exotic inventions distilled from the particular source that had captured their imagination.

After the foundations of Art Nouveau were laid down in England developments of it spread over Europe and to America, and although the First World War halted its progress its influence continued. In its debased form it flooded the market of a growing middle-class eager for change with mass-produced ugliness. At its best, Art Nouveau was a purely decorative movement of great vitality, transforming, re-creating and changing the old classical values to a re-styled view of nature, preoccupied with abstraction, curvilinear rhythms and the "scientific" look.

Collectors of foresight have been interested in this movement for some time, and sale prices continue to rise. But do remember that selection is even more important in looking for good pieces of Art Nouveau. Those that concern the Victoriana collector are, strictly speaking, ones that were made in the 1880s and 1890s. However, as I have said elsewhere, for a collector to keep too scrupulously within his period is to defeat his own ends. A study of past influences and future developments will enrich his understanding of his chosen epoch.

At first a cry of "decadent" was levelled at many poets and artists of Art Nouveau both in England and elsewhere. Wilde and Swinburne, Mallarmé and Verlaine are examples, as well as, of course, the haunting and rather unhealthy drawings of Aubrey Beardsley, with their Japanese-inspired neurotic atmosphere.

But what a wealth of new, imaginative work we find. Look for those dreamy, *fin-de-siècle* nymphs on silver and pewter dishes and picture-frames or vases made by British, German and French artists. There was a great silver content in the pewter used at this time and the material polishes to a beautiful sheen. Green and blue enamel was used to decorate silver or pewter.

Art Nouveau's direct ancestor was the Arts and Crafts movement associated with the name of William Morris, who was a friend of Rosetti and Burne-Jones. He was the first to try to improve industrial design, and his taste for simplicity and an unaffected, straightforward style was a strong influence on Art Nouveau artists who followed him. There has been a revival of interest in Morris's wallpapers and textile designs recently.

Collectors of glass of this period look for the work of Emile Gallé of Nancy. He had his own pottery workshop and by 1880 was also experimenting with Oriental decorations for glassware, subsequently using layers of glass to give beautiful shades of soft red, yellow-green, lemon-yellow, orange and violet-blue, all against a greyish white background. He also designed furniture, employing a vast number of skilled workmen in all his enterprises. In spite of this form of mass-production his glass pieces look absolutely individual.

In the 1890s such French artists as Edouard Villard and Pierre Bonnard worked for an art shop kept by S. Bing in Paris, and also made stained glass for Louis Comfort Tiffany's shop in New York. Tiffany's Favrile glass, patented in 1880, is especially lovely, a flowering of strange botanical forms in brilliant greens, reds and yellows. Tiffany, the son of a fashionable American jeweller, had studied painting in Paris and then experimented in glass from 1875.

René Lalique is associated with fabulous flower-inspired jewellery as well as his glass and silver masterpieces. French Art Nouveau jewellery is quite outstanding.

Arthur Lazenby Liberty, in London, was another of the three shop owners who were all influential in spreading the gospel of Art Nouveau and who were also themselves collectors, mostly of Oriental treasures.

For those interested in exploring this particular side of Victorian antiques I recommend strongly a small book by Mario Amaya, called *Art Nouveau*, published in Dutton's Vista Pictureback series. It is of course impossible to give more than an appetizing foretaste of this fascinating subject in so small a compass.

The Victoria and Albert Museum has a botanical extravaganza of a brass coat-rack made about 1895, and a silver porringer set with semi-precious stones, dated *c.* 1900. Those interested in small items may easily find picture-frames, pen-trays, ink-wells, jewellery, glass, pewter, silver and even dolls' houses inspired by this movement in art. I have myself a charming pair of miniature garden chairs made of silver-laden pewter, which stand outside an 1895 dolls' house boasting a wallpaper with the curves and circles beloved by Art Nouveau artists.

One comfort for collectors is that they will find it extremely easy to pick out examples of this strangely appealing, very individual style. Whether they pick the best is, of course, a matter of taste, and that is one thing that cannot be taught.

10

Stevens' Woven Silk Pictures

In 1854 Thomas Stevens, who had been in the trade of weaving silks for most of his life, set up on his own. The initial weaving of silk ribbons began in Coventry as early as 1700, which perhaps we tend to forget. As far as we are concerned, however, the famous Coventry ribbons are associated in our minds with the reign of Queen Victoria and the name of Thomas Stevens.

He was a great innovator, always interested in experimenting and improving methods of production, and in spite of a terrible slump in the 1860s, when our market was suddenly flooded with cheap ribbons from the Continent, Stevens' factory carried on. He had adapted the famous Jacquard loom to his purposes and in 1863 he sold his first bookmarker.

Though this may well have fluttered a few female hearts, for the period was still that of the gifted amateur, home-made objects being the pastime of every girl in the schoolroom as well as her leisured elders, the new venture found great favour. Before long, booksellers were marketing these attractive novelties which celebrated contemporary events and noteworthy public figures as well as offering Bible verses and birthday or seasonal sentiments to readers. These charming little pictures were, as we have seen, the stock in trade of booksellers rather than drapers, and perhaps it was here that Stevens was original once more. Up until now, as was to be expected, ribbons and brocades were sold at the draper's shop only. There were not only bookmarkers, Christmas and birthday greeting cards, Valentines and calendars with their woven pictures and poems, but also sashes, badges and later, in 1879, the first Stevengraph pictures, ready mounted for framing and hanging charmingly on the parlour walls. These appeared to please an enormous public. Literally thousands of the woven pictures were sold, their only fault being, alas, that they are sensitive to sunlight and therefore fade.

Stevens moved to London and looked after his thriving business there while his two sons kept the factory going at Coventry. He died in 1888 but the family kept the business on for another twenty years when it was formed into a company and flourished until the Second World War finally put an end to this enormously successful firm's life. It was bombed beyond recovery during the Coventry blitz.

Austin Sprake is the expert to whom all Coventry ribbon addicts defer. His book,[1] written in collaboration with Mr Michael Darby, is an essential for a serious collector, listing as it does all the known pictures and book markers, giving invaluable information about their identification, size and colours and tips for those wishing to display their collection so that the colours don't fade through sunshine or perish with damp.

Many of the pictures are fairly common. The portrait of *Queen Victoria*, *Queen Alexandra* and *Edward VII* are easy to find, though the *Prince of Wales* (later Edward VII) is rare, especially the one with the portrait facing ahead with flags below. Equally, *Queen Victoria* is common in her Jubilee portrait facing right, as well as the one entitled *"Her Majesty Queen Victoria, Queen of an Empire on which the sun never sets"*. Others of the Queen are rare.

Again, all the "notables and sportsmen" are more or less rare, and so are the "Religious, Classical and Historical portraits", of which, perhaps, *Leda and the Swan* is fetching the highest price today.

The appeal of these little pictures to the Victoriana collector is very simply that they are a mirror of the age. Suppose, for instance, you decide to collect Exhibitions only, then here you will find representations of England, America, Scotland and Belgium with an

[1] *Stevengraphs* (privately printed, 1968).

absolutely authentic period flavour. The same applies to castles, buildings and views and bridges. You will delight in the fire-engines, coaches, the trains of the period, sports, battleships and boats, military portraits, the pictures of famous jockeys and so on. If you are thinking of building up a picture of the age, here is your best choice. But don't expect to find these little treasures for nothing. Some were fetching as much as £210 in 1968.

There were others who manufactured ribbons, following in Stevens' footsteps, and the French firm of Grangier Frères et Ogier produced a collectable ribbon celebrating the victory of England and France over the Russians at the Battle of Alma in 1854. This is in black and white except for the flags and the scalloped border of green. Stevens' chief competitor in this field was the English firm of W. H. Grant, also from Coventry. Mr Sprake considers this firm was inferior to Stevens. Since they produced some military and royal portraits it is just as well to be careful not to acquire a Grant when you thought you had a Stevens. Mr Sprake's book lists some of the subjects that Grant made in about the same size as those of Stevens. They are, however, not very numerous.

Finally, it goes without saying that brilliance of colour is the quality we look for, and mounts with trade labels or with descriptive labels. It is possible to date the Stevengraphs from the trade labels approximately, as the earliest had only one subject listed and dated 1879, whereas those with several titles are probably about 1880–81.

As a footnote, an unusual item appeared in a sale catalogue of Stevengraphs in September 1969: the portrait of *Queen Victoria, Queen of an Empire on which the sun never sets* was incorporated in a ladies' companion, complete with bodkins and other necessities, and inside was *The Crystal Palace* (Interior) Stevengraph. It was considered to be unique. Well, Stevengraphs may well be lurking in other unexpected places.

11

Victorian Oddities and the Great Exhibition

The Great Exhibition of 1851 must be something that springs at once to the mind of every collector of Victoriana. The very building itself was extraordinary and unique. In a sense it was the birthplace of that ancestor of our splendid Victoria and Albert Museum, the Ornamental Art Collection of the South Kensington Museum. It was the Prince Consort's brain-child, of course, and the outstanding success of his life. Appealing to all classes of people, this gigantic enterprise was of great value to the country educationally and produced the colossal profit of £186,000. One of the purchases out of this money was the site in Kensington for Prince Albert's dearest plan, a cultural and educational centre for Londoners and, indeed, for everybody else.

The 1851 Crystal Palace, which held the enormous trade fair we associate with Victorian days, was to be the forerunner of our modern industrial exhibitions. It may come as a surprise to some of us to recall that a display of manufactured wares, with prizes awarded for specially noteworthy pieces, took place in London as long ago as 1756. The French followed suit nearly half a century later, and this has become an institution in France.

Paxton's enormous palace of glass was designed to house three gigantic elms nobody wanted to destroy. In spite of the gloomiest prognostications of disaster the building was triumphantly erected by an eventual 2,112 workmen by January 1851, having been begun in

September 1850 with only 39 men. There were at least 18,000 panes of glass in the roof of the nave alone.

The commemorative album of the Great Exhibition prepared by the Victoria and Albert Museum in 1951 picked out a splendid assortment of strange things on view as well as the comments of some of those attending the Crystal Palace. It seems Queen Victoria was much entertained by the story of an unfortunate wig-maker who was expecting to be included under the "Fine Arts" and found to his dismay that he was relegated to the stand showing "Animal Products". The famous story of the flock of sparrows is recalled. Living happily in the huge elms, they were no respecters of either exhibits or persons. What could be done? Shooting was out of the question. With admirable commonsense the Duke of Wellington solved the problem: "Try sparrow-hawks, Ma'am," he advised the Queen. It worked.

Whether present-day collectors will be able to discover any of the remarkable oddities shown at the Exhibition is uncertain. They might look for the patent ventilating hats that had a valve in the crown which could be opened and shut at will "to allow the perspiration to escape". Other sartorial surprises were the cuffs knitted from wool that was plucked from the backs of French poodles and hand-spun. Or there was a splendid pair of trousers, "so arranged that they remain as a fixture to the heel without straps and dispense with braces". Another pair of trousers could be worn in three different ways, "either as a French bottom, or gaiters attached, or plain bottom with improvements". That would be worth finding. Then there was a dressing-table which became a fire-escape at a moment's notice; and a Registered Alarum bedstead, which collapsed beneath the heavy sleeper "without any jerk or the slightest personal danger", setting him on his feet in the middle of the room. The Official Catalogue adds, unsmilingly, that a cold bath can be placed ready "at the option of the possessor . . . to ensure his being rendered rapidly wide-awake". How many of these survive?

There was also an Asiatic style fountain, complete with three statues, which could be neatly converted into a fireplace in winter.

Queen Victoria probably viewed the above-mentioned exhibits unamused, but she did find considerable entertainment from the stuffed animals shown by Hermann Plouquet of Würtemberg, particularly the frog shaving his companion.

Pugin designed a huge stove "in mediaeval style" which looks like a bastard Milan Cathedral. Another stove came from Prussia; characteristically it was in the form of an enormous knight in armour standing on a pseudo-Gothic looking base made of cast-iron.

I found a few curious objects not long ago that would have fitted into the 1851 Exhibition very well, had they been invented as early as that. Victorian they are, but of a later date. One is a silver plated ear-trumpet, which looks like a musical instrument at first glance; another is a brass needlecase like a butterfly, made by Redditch; a miniature version of a folding harmonium, such as those used at Revivalists' open-air meetings; and there is also a grisly inkwell, made from an albatross's head, that would have frightened the Ancient Mariner into fits.

There are certainly many more of these strange inspirations of the nineteenth century waiting to be found by collectors searching for something out of the normal run.

12

Workbox Treasure-trove

In Victorian days the ladies of the household occupied themselves with "every description of Plain and Ornamental Needlework" and so a number of shops began to trade in "Everything for the work-table", until by 1873 Pontings opened in Kensington High Street specializing in everything to do with "the practice of art needlework".

In the early years of the century there were plenty of market-stalls selling haberdashery and drapery and the sight of a travelling "lace-man" was quite common. He would probably offer the French ribbons which fashionable ladies made use of freely, and "French tulle garni-tures", as well as the tiffanies and waddings, the bugle fringes, gold and silver tissues and gauze satin and crêpe flowers to sew on hats or bonnets, caps or turbans. Many of the best trimmings came over from France even in spite of the Napoleonic Wars. Jane Austen, writing to her sister Cassandra, discusses the "whim-whams and fribble-frabble of fashion" and talks about the "gowns" she bought. In fact, this meant the length of material to make a gown. There was always the visiting dressmaker or the sewing-woman in the village who could make this up into a fashionable garment, following a style in one of the monthly fashion magazines.

The nineteenth-century needlewoman had a wealth of delightful accessories to her workbox. Up to the 1850s every stitch had to be worked by hand, until the first Singer sewing-machine crossed the Atlantic from America to Glasgow. True, a French tailor invented a similar machine as early as 1829, and he exhibited one in the Great

Exhibition of 1851, but this innovation only slowly entered the average home, and even to this day the preference for hand-sewn articles remains rooted in most women's hearts, except, of course, for those long weary seams that were so exquisitely worked by our ancestors. Go to the costume hall in the Victoria and Albert Museum, or to Bath's Assembly Rooms with their splendid array of clothes and underwear. This will give you some idea of the tasks people cheerfully undertook in the pre-machine age. The stitches, the embroidery, the elaborate fringes and tassels and pearls, beads and other decorations which make the early clothes so desirable were all done by hand.

It is quite easy to find nineteenth-century workboxes, but nearly always these beautiful leather, wood, *papier-mâché* and mother-of-pearl boxes have been rifled of their accessories. Occasionally we come across one of those charming Sheraton-style workboxes in the shape of a piano, often fitted with a musical box which sings as the lid is opened. This is generally fitted with its original silver scissors and stiletto, thimble, tweezers to pick up beads, a needlecase and so forth. One of the most popular treasures is the walnut, lined in velvet and trimmed with ormulu, fitted up with diminutive thimble, scissors and other useful objects.

In the trays of oddments that some antique dealers obligingly put out for us to hunt about in there are often amusing little pieces for our empty workbox. You may be lucky enough to find a patchwork pincushion, embellished by those brilliant blue beads, a beadwork scissor or needlecase, a pin-poppet the size of a thimble used for keeping pins in, or some of those pretty thread winders made of wood, ivory or mother-of-pearl. Some of them look like magnified snowflakes in shape.

Needleholders are in great variety. They are often in the shape of an umbrella made out of bone, ivory or wood, and even out of silver. Sometimes we find bean pods in the same materials. These, too, kept needles safe and are quite a miracle of workmanship, the stalk end fitting impeccably on to the pod. Some lovely holders, earlier than our period, were formed into little figurines.

Thread-winders, in use before the days of cotton reels, are in many amusing shapes. The reel itself, with the cotton ready wound on it, was replacing the early shapes by early Victorian days, but the needlewomen, used to the pretty shapes of earlier times, used ornamental reel-holders for many years.

Thimbles are, of course, collectors' items in themselves, and have been for some time. They were found in the ruins of cities like Pompeii and Herculaneium and Elizabeth I owned a number of very costly thimbles. In Victorian days an amusing type of thimble with relief pictures of famous landmarks was made for the tourist trade. You may find thimbles made of bronze, of gold and silver; there are mother-of-pearl ones from France, glass, wood, and ivory ones; perhaps best of all are the lovely Battersea and Bilston enamel examples and even china ones. Thimble cases, too, are in all sorts of shapes. Eggs and acorns are the most popular.

Another quarry is the yard measure, and here again ingenuity thought up any number of different shapes: acorns, cylinders, baskets, bells, eggs and beehives for a start. The materials are legion, too: Tunbridge ware, ivory, shells, wood, ebony and silver are all popular.

There is no doubt that anyone with an attractive workbox or workbox table will have endless opportunity for filling it with delightful, beautifully made objects from pincushions to châtelaines and from winding clamps and sewing-clamps of intricate designs to elaborate scissors, powder-sprinklers, wax boxes, darning eggs and hand-coolers. The difference, by the way, between the last two objects is that the darning egg is always made of a light material, whereas hand-coolers could be of any heavy natural stone, especially poor conductors of heat like marble. Glove darning sticks are normally of wood with two round, acornlike knobs on each end of a short rod.

Generally a small scent-bottle is included in every workbox and this, Sylvia Groves tells us, was for removing the grease from fingers.

Anyone interested in the absorbing subject of needlework tools should read *The History of Needlework Tools and Accessories* by Sylvia Groves.

13

Silhouettes

The true silhouette, a profile cut out by a pair of fine scissors, owes its name to a certain minister of Louis XV's. In 1757 the King asked M. Etienne de Silhouette to take over the formidable task of reducing State expenditure by half; it caused a French wit to suggest giving the minister's name to the very cheap art of making likenesses. The side or profile was therefore called a silhouette, which quickly became common usage.

It was no doubt due to the inexpensiveness of profile portraiture, compared to the price of a portrait in oils or a bust in marble, that it lasted so long—from the middle of the eighteenth century to about 1850.

The most famous artist of the true silhouette after 1825 was Augustin Edouart. Since the Victorian Age customarily is supposed to begin from the date of the Reform Bill in 1832, Edouart is safely within our range.

Most people would agree that the Georgian profile artists were the finest and that once Queen Victoria came to the throne the art began to deteriorate. This, however, was not the case as far as the French refugee Augustin Edouart was concerned. He came to England in 1815 when he was twenty-six years old and tried to eke out an existence teaching French. After modelling in wax, chiefly dog portraits, he experimented in scissor-cutting and soon made a great success of this deft-fingered craft. He is believed to have cut no less than a quarter of a million profiles, some of which were mounted on a hand-painted background and some on lithographs, others being simply the black profile portrait of his sitter pasted on to a plain white card. He charged five shillings for full-length portraits and seven shillings if the subject was seated. For profiles of celebrated people of his day he charged three shillings apiece. At the same time the art of scissor profiles had become popular and cheap and his contemporaries offered likenesses to customers on Brighton pier and elsewhere for threepence and sixpence with coloured versions for one and sixpence, on the time-honoured principle of "penny plain and twopence coloured".

Edouart moved round England, Scotland and Ireland practising his craft in fashionable resorts and soon became celebrated and much in demand. His conversation-pieces featuring the whole family are especially delightful, and one useful point is that he signed most of his work. He was not one of the profilists who gilded or painted his cut-outs as other artists used to do. Edward Foster (1762–1864) made his portraits in a pleasant Indian-red touched with gold, for example. Another well-known scissor-cutter called William Hubard (1807–62) also used gold for heightening his effects and is noted for his charming landscapes cut out with tiny figures, which, in fact, were meant to be pasted into the fashionable scrap-books of the times.

The more elaborate silhouettes during the hey-day of this delicate art are outside our scope but we should consider silhouette jewellery, another offshoot of the craft. These exquisite little profiles enriched mourning-rings, brooches, pins and small boxes for cachous, patches or snuff and began to become the vogue early in the nineteenth century.

After having written an erudite book called *Treatise on Silhouette Likenesses* in 1835, Edouart ventured out to America. There must be many examples of his work in that country for he stayed there for ten years. He seems not to have done very much after 1850 and died in France, to where he eventually retired, in 1861.

Collectors may be interested in the frames of silhouettes which were used at different times. In the Victorian period either pearwood or bird's eye maplewood with mitred corners were used, while in the early nineteenth century black *papier-mâché* with the typical acorn-ring hangers was in favour.

Although the art of scissor-cutting lingered on in parlour pastimes, Louis Daguerre's process known as daguerreotype sounded the death knell to profile portraits and photography took its place as the cheapest form of making likenesses.

A collage picture made by a court tailor named G. Smart from Sussex; the hussar lifts up and lowers his shako

A workbox in a walnut shell, mid-nineteenth century

Lady's Companion, pin-box with landscape, hand-shaped necklace clip, enamel button, thimbles, shoe needlecase and gilt shoe pin-box

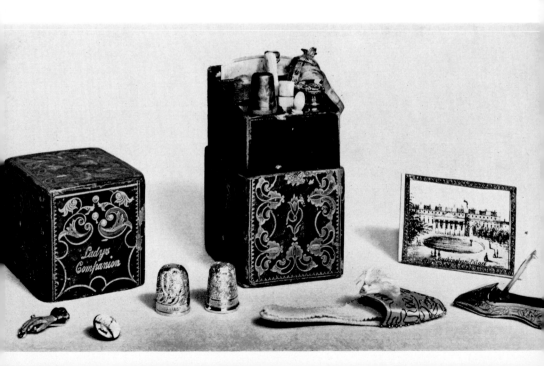

CARE OF YOUR COLLECTION

The care of your antiques is as important as their acquisition and one or two final hints are worth offering.

If you require restoration work, do go to a professional in repairs of your particular class of object. So often home repairs are a catastrophe and do irretrievable damage. If possible, of course, buy goods that are perfect. For one thing should you wish to part with one of your pieces on some later occasion, you will find it extremely difficult to sell cracked or repaired antiques.

Treat your antiques with respect, remembering that old materials, prints or water-colours as well as furniture fade in strong light. Central heating can crack and warp wood, so invest in humidifiers to keep the air moist. Insect pests such as woodworm thrive in dust and dirt on the wood they bore into and enjoy a bit of damp too. Three-ply wood is their favourite meal. Treat the holes drastically with one of the brands of liquid available and do it again a year later, then keep an eye on it every Spring in case even one destructive beetle has been overlooked.

Wash glass very carefully in warm water with a little weak detergent and if possible do each piece separately, rinsing with cooler water and finally cold. A soft linen towel is best for drying—not cotton, which leaves tiresome pieces of fluff behind. Decanters should not be put away with the stopper in and remember never to use strong bleaches on old china or pottery.

Remember, too, that old bone and ivory are both badly affected by heat and will become warped and distorted. The disastrous effect of heat on wax dolls isn't likely to be overlooked and extremes of temperature, hot or cold, are bad for them.

Fabrics are not so likely to attract moths if cleaned and, of course, one use for those plastic food bags is to keep materials clean and damp-proof.

A last word. Remember that when forming a collection it's as well not to be absolutely rigid over what you include. Something a few years earlier than your chosen period will point to the origin of a trend or fashion. Something a few years too late may give an interesting foretaste of decline or emergence of new tastes.

The old cliché about the dangers of a little knowledge is overdone in the world of antiques. Here it is better to know something than nothing at all, so the more you look in museums, the more friends you make in good antique shops and with seasoned collectors and the more you read specialist books the better. To this end a select bibliography has been included, and do remember it is select.

Some Museums to Visit

Bangor, Caernarvon: Penrhyn Castle.
Bath, Somerset: American Museum in Britain; Museum of Costume, The Assembly Rooms.
Birmingham, Warks: Museum and Art Gallery.
Bristol, Somerset: City Museum.
Cardiff: National Museum of Wales.
Exmouth, Devon: A la Ronde, near Exmouth.
Cambridge: Cambridge and County Folk Museum.
Castleford, Yorks: Castleford Museum.
Cheltenham, Glos: Cheltenham Museum.
Edinburgh: Museum of Childhood.
Glamis, Scotland: Angus Folk Collection, Kirkwynd.
Glandford, Norfolk: Shell Museum.
Henbury, Nr. Bristol: Grange Art Gallery and Museum.
High Wycombe, Bucks: The Museum and Art Gallery.
Hove, Sussex: Hove Museum of Art.
Ipswich, Suffolk: Christchurch Museum.
Isle of Wight: Arreton Manor; Osborne House.
Kirkstall, Leeds: Abbey House Museum.
Newport, Monmouthshire: Newport Museum.
Norwich, Norfolk: Strangers' Hall.
London: Bethnal Green Museum; Dickens House; Geffrye Museum; London Museum; Pollocks' Toy Museum; Science Museum; Victoria and Albert Museum.
Oxford: The Rotunda Museum of Dolls' Houses.
Peterborough, Northamptonshire: Peterborough Museum, Priestgate.
Preston, Lancs: Harris Art Gallery and Museum.
Rottingdean, Sussex: Grange Art Gallery and Museum.
Royal Tunbridge Wells, Kent: The Royal Tunbridge Wells Museum.
Rugely, Staffs: Museum of Childhood and Costume, Blithfield Hall.

Salisbury, Wilts: The Museum.
Sheffield: City Museum.
Stoke-on-Trent, Staffs: Spode-Copeland Museum.
Taunton, Somerset: Somerset County Museum, Taunton Castle.
Warwick: Doll Museum.
West Hoathly, Sussex: The Priests' House.
Wonersh, Surrey: The Sharp Collection.
Worthing, Sussex: Worthing Museum and Art Gallery.
York: York Castle Museum.
(This is only a beginning. There are many other museums, and also the stately homes.)

Selected Bibliography for Further Reading

AMAYA, MARIO: *Art Nouveau* (Studio Vista, Dutton Paperbacks, 1966).

BALSTON, THOMAS: *Staffordshire Portrait Figures of the Victorian Age* (Faber & Faber Ltd., 1958).

BERGSTROM, EVANGELINE H.: *Old Glass Paperweights* (Crown Publishers, New York, 1940).

COLEMAN, D. S., E. A., and E. J.: *The Collector's Encyclopaedia of Dolls* (Robert Hale & Co., 1970).

ELVILLE, E. M.: *The Collectors' Dictionary of Glass* (Country Life, 1961).

GIBBS-SMITH, C. H.: *The Great Exhibition of 1851* (commemorative album) (Her Majesty's Stationery Office, 1951).

GLOAG, JOHN: *A Short Dictionary of Furniture* (George Allen & Unwin Ltd., 1952).

GREENE, VIVIEN: *English Dolls' Houses of the 18th and 19th Centuries* (B. T. Batsford, 1955).

HAGGAR, REGINALD G.: *English Country Pottery* (Phoenix House Ltd., 1950).

HILLIER, MARY: *Pageant of Toys* (Elek Books, 1965).

HUGHES, G. BERNARD: *Collecting Antiques* (revised edition) (Country Life, 1960).

JACOBS, FLORA GILL and FAURHOLT, ESTRID: *Dolls and Dolls' Houses* (Charles E. Tuttle Co., 1967).

LAMBERT, M. and MARX, ENID: *English Popular Art* (B. T. Batsford Ltd., 1951).

LATHAM, JEAN: *Dolls' Houses: A Personal Choice.* (A. & C. Black Ltd., 1969).

LAVER, JAMES: *Victoriana* (Ward Lock & Co., 1966).

MURRAY, PATRICK: *Toys* (Studio Vista, Dutton Paperbacks, 1968).

NOBLE, JOHN: *Dolls* (Walker & Co., New York, 1967).

RABECQ-MAILLARD, M.-M.: *Histoire du Jouet* (Hachette, 1962).

SPRAKE, AUSTIN, and DARBY, MICHAEL: *Stevengraphs* (privately printed 1968).

STANLEY, LOUIS T.: *Collecting Staffordshire Pottery* (W. H. Allen, 1963).

TOLLER, JANE: *Antique Miniature Furniture* (G. Bell & Sons Ltd., 1966).

WOOD, VIOLET: *Victoriana* (G. Bell & Sons Ltd., 1960).

YARWOOD, DOREEN: *The English Home* (B. T. Batsford Ltd., 1956).

The Bryant and May Museum of Fire-making Appliances catalogue, 1926.

INDEX

Index

Caxton, William, 97
chairs, 126–8
chandeliers, 104
châtelaines, 113
Chisholme, Emma, 86
churchwarden pipes, 120
cigar holders, 122
cigarettes, 121, 123
cigars, 120–1
Clarke, Samuel, 105
clay pipes, 120
Coalport pottery, 15, 17, 95
Cole, Archibald, 106
Colin, Alexandre Marie, 84
collages, 89
companion chairs, 127
Compte-Calix, F. C., 84
Conta and Boehme, 33, 98
Corday, Charlotte, 18
Corder, William, 17
cork pictures, 85
cosmetics, 112
cottages, pottery, 15–18
cow-creamers, pottery, 29
Crane, Walter, 129
Crystal Palace, 136
Curiosities of Glass-making (Pellatt), 68

Daguerre, Louis-Jacques-Mandé, 112, 144
daguerrotypes, 11, 112, 144
Darby, Michael, 134
Darling, Grace, 38
darning eggs, 141
Derby pottery, 15, 17, 95, 105
d'Estrée, Gabrielle, 79

deutsch ("dutch") dolls, 46, 47, 85
Devis, Jeanette, 86
Diamond Sutra, 97
Dickens, Charles, 11, 36
divan easy chairs, 127
dolls, 40–50; baby, 45–6; "bagman's", 44; *bisque*, 45, 46; *deutsch* ("dutch"), 46, 47, 85; fashion, 43–4; fortune-telling, 49; Jumeau, 46–7, 114; kitchen, 52–3; pedlar, 47, 48–50; pegwooden, 47, 90, 99, 108; rolypoly, 64; wax, 47
dolls' houses, 51–3, 107, 108–9
dolls' house shades, 76
dolls' shops, 53—4
domino-boxes, 94
Don Pottery, 21, 29
doorstops, 17; lion, 25
double-chairs, 127
dressing tables, 112–5
duplex burners, 104
"dutch" dolls, *see deutsch* dolls

earthenware, 19
Edouart, Augustin, 142–3
electric lighting, 104–5
Elizabeth I, Queen, 79
Englishwoman's Domestic Magazine, 82
essence pots, 16
European and American Dolls (White), 50
Ewart, Henrietta, 86

fakes, 18, 50, 128
Family Friend, The, 85–6

scissors, 101, 113
scrimshaw work, 116
seals, 99, 101
sewing-machines, 139–40
shades, glass, 73–7
shellwork, 74–5, 90–1
Sherratt, Obadiah, 29
ships-in-bottles, 116, 118
shoes: brass, 93; glass, 93, 95; pewter, 93; pottery, 93; stoneware, 95; wooden, 93–4
Shop Hours Act (1886), 13
silhouettes, 142–4
silk pictures, 133–5
skirt clips, 113
slagware, 72
Smith, William, & Co., 21
snuff, 121
snuff boxes, 93, 94
soldiers, toy, 62
songsheets, 13
spirit flasks, 95
Spode, Josiah II, 95
Spode pottery, 15
Sprake, Austin, 134–5
Staffordshire pottery, 16, 17, 24, 25, 27–8, 29–30, 36–9
Staffordshire pottery figures, 55
"Stanbrig Eorls", 51
standard lamps, 105
standishes, 98–9
Stanfield Hall, 17
statuettes, *see* pottery figures
stay-busks, 117
steatite, 78
Stevengraph pictures, 134–5
Stevens, Thomas, 133–4

Stoke Porcelain, 95
Strawberry Hill, 15
string-boxes, 101
student lamps, 103–4
stump-work, 80, 115

Talbot, Fox, 112
tampers, 123
tea-caddies, 17
teapots, 17, 24
theatres, toy, 55–6
theorem paintings, 87
thimbles, 141
thread-winders, 141
Tiffany, Louis Comfort, 70, 105, 131
tinder-boxes, 123
tinsel pictures, 55–6, 86
tobacco, 120–1
tobacco boxes, 123
tobacco jars, 17, 24
toilet boxes, 113
Tommy Thumb's Pretty Song-book, 19
Toudouze, Anaïs, 84
toy furniture, 108–11
toy soldiers, 62
toy theatres, 55
toys, 40–2, 62–5; clockwork, 65; moving, 64–5
Treatise on Silhouette Likenesses (Edouart), 143
Tuhten, Frank, & Co., 33
Turpin, Dick, 36

Valentines, 91, 117
Van de Velde, Willem, 25
vases, glass, 71

INDEX